SHIFT

how to reinvent your business,
your career, and your personal brand

PETER ARNELL

with Steve Kettmann

BROADWAY BOOKS
NEW YORK

BROADWAY

Copyright © 2010 by Peter Eric Arnell
All rights reserved.

Published in the United States by Broadway Books,
an imprint of the Crown Publishing Group,
a division of Random House, Inc., New York.
www.crownpublishing.com

Photographs courtesy of Peter Arnell with the following
exceptions: photo of Peter Arnell and Bob Nardelli next to
Peapod car, which is by David Kennerly, and the photo of
Peter Arnell and Muhammad Ali, which is by Jack Ader

Library of Congress Cataloging-in-Publication Data
Arnell, Peter.
   Shift : how to reinvent your business, your career, and your
personal brand / Peter Arnell ; with Steve Kettmann. — 1st ed.
      p. cm.
   1. Organizational change. 2. Change (Psychology). 3. Branding
(Marketing). I. Kettmann, Steve. II. Title.

HD58.8.A756 2010
650.1—dc22
                                        2009048076

ISBN 978-0-385-52627-2

Printed in the United States of America
10 9 8 7 6 5 4 3 2 1

First Edition

For my family

Contents

Part Two
Tactics That Work

You need dreams to live. It's as essential as a road to walk on and as bread to eat. I would have felt myself dying if this dream would have been taken away from me by reason.

P H I L I P P E   P E T I T

*Reflecting on his high-wire walk between
the World Trade Center towers on August 7, 1974*

Foreword by Martha Stewart

PETER ARNELL IS ALL ABOUT A LOT OF THINGS. He creates. He thinks. He learns. He teaches. He invents. And he reinvents.

Few of us do as much in a lifetime as Peter can do in a decade. Give him two decades, or three, and the productivity—the changes wrought, the new things envisioned, the fresh ideas devised, the unthinkable accomplishments—is mindboggling.

The original and authentic work that Peter and his companies have so beautifully created—the branding, the products, the reimaging, the experiences, the environments—is legendary in fashion, electronics, automotive, and consumer marketing and manufacturing. And now Peter has added a new dimension to his work: the personal shifting of the man—himself.

Always an avid student, an inveterate researcher, and a passionate collector, Peter focuses his attention in this book on what one can do oneself that will change forever one's personal "landscape," in order to live a better, more fulfilling, more interesting, and more balanced existence. Famous for the "extreme," Peter has written how he has turned that penchant for the extreme into a positive and new direction for a different kind of life, while never sacrificing his quest for being the best.

If it meant learning how to "invent" a dietary regimen based on consuming an extreme number of oranges and quantities of raw fish and vegetables in order to shed more than 256 pounds, then Peter learned.

If it meant defying all the odds by "inventing" the Peapod, a new type of car that would use far less fuel and leave a much smaller "carbon footprint," or HomeHero, an eco-friendly fire extinguisher, then Peter defied them.

If it meant adapting to a new lifestyle and living it every day in order to cope with weight loss, a much leaner body, and a new wardrobe of beautiful clothing, then Peter adapted.

Shift is about Peter's business acumen. It's about extreme thinking with practical applications. It's about taking what is there and mixing it all up and emerging with something so much better, so much more modern, so much more useful and sensible, that one cannot imagine that anything different was ever there in the first place.

Shift is an idea that everyone can use. It's about moving forward, not looking backward, and changing for the better and forever.

Good luck with your own Shift!
Martha Stewart

Part One
Branding Ourselves

Introduction

Italy, August 2009

A room service waiter walked into my room. He brought me a big bowl of navel oranges, as I requested. A few hours later, he came back with another bowl of oranges, which I had also requested. He asked why I ate so many oranges, so I told him how I lost 256 pounds and changed things about myself as a person that were making me unhappy. Every day he brought me my bowl of oranges, on multiple occasions. Then, one day, he told me that he had started eating oranges himself. He was already thin and didn't look like he needed to lose weight, so I asked him why he started eating oranges. He said, "Everyone can use some change for the better in life. So since oranges work for you and make you happy, I thought I would try them, too." By the time my stay at that hotel was over, the waiter said he was feeling "*buonissimo.*"

CHAPTER I

Start Your Own Orange Revolution

IT ALL STARTED with oranges. Many oranges.

If I were to reach out right now to shake your hand, you would probably be surprised to see the color of my hands. People always stare at the deep orange glow my hands give off. It's a loud, warm orange, not a color that anyone expects to see on someone's hands. But since I look fit and trim and healthy, people usually just wonder, ask nicely, or shrug it off. Fact is, my hands are orange-colored because for years I have been peeling and eating as many as fifty oranges a day.

I can't pinpoint the moment I went orange and set about transforming myself and changing my life. As much as I talk about oranges as if they were part of a careful plan, the truth is that I started eating a lot of oranges mostly because I liked the way they tasted, they were available anywhere in the world, and I liked the way peeling and eating an orange kept

15

me focused. The oranges became a ritual as much as a healthy snack. They became almost a touchstone for change. I knew I was 100 percent serious about transforming myself, and eating many, many oranges, from all over the world—in season, out of season, organic, or conventional—helped me keep on track.

Wherever I go, I strike up conversations about all the oranges I carry around with me; I also get some of the most curious looks. In a business meeting, walking around, traveling, driving in the car, or watching TV, I always have oranges with me. I carry them in a small wicker basket or paper bag, which never fails to elicit the question "What's in there?" They get everyone talking and are a great way to open up a conversation. Oranges have become my symbol for change. Now, when people I know visit me, they bring me oranges. For my birthday, holidays, thank-yous, greetings, and all other kinds of reasons, friends send me bags and boxes of oranges. On the road in various far-off cities, while other travelers find themselves welcomed in their hotel rooms with bottles of wine or champagne or baskets full of crackers and chocolate-covered strawberries, I am welcomed by a big beautiful bowl of oranges.

When I plan my travel to cities where I need to go, I think about the great places I have discovered where I can load up on the best oranges—Whole Foods in L.A., Sembikiya in Tokyo, Fauchon in Paris, Peck in Milan, Harrods Food Court in London, and Chelsea Market in New York. On long international flights, I bring as many as fifty oranges. Usually I can't eat all of them, so at the end, I offer some to the flight attendants, who seem to love them. When I show up to see my friend Frank Gehry, the architect, at his office in L.A., his staff announces me as "Orange Man."

I'm constantly peeling oranges. But truth be told, the oranges peeled me as well. That's what they've done for a long time. They peeled away layers within me. They convinced me that I could *change*. That I didn't have to remain the way I was—a 400-plus-pound man in what should have been a 150-pound body. Of course, I'm not forgetting the physicality of the oranges—the vitamins they contain, their sweetness, and their acidity. But they are far more than food to me. Oranges have become a talisman, a touchstone. They delivered me from my previous life, from the hope and disappointment that accompanied my earlier efforts to lose weight. They helped to give me back my 150-pound body.

As a result, I've never gotten tired of the taste of oranges. To me, orange is the flavor of freedom. It is the taste of being on the right track. Oranges are a tangible manifestation of the power of change, of my ability to overturn my old habits, and of my approach to life. I needed that tangible, physical manifestation of change. And so, I would argue, does anyone who wants to effect profound change in his or her life.

But this is not a diet book.

This is a book about human transformation. It is based on business strategies and tactics that mainstream brands apply to stay relevant with consumers. It takes those strategies, puts them in a personal context, and shows you how to brand yourself to be the best you can be. It shows how you can achieve Shift—a slight move in your attitude, in your thinking, in your behavior, or your life.

As cosmetic surgery can reshape your physical features, the idea of Shift can reshape and enhance your image and identity and beliefs to help you brand yourself a better person. It can help you manage and take control of how you are perceived by the world around you. Consumer brands do this everyday through their advertising, Web sites, products, and packaging, and through the people, places, and events they associate with. You can achieve your own results by learning to apply brand-building strategies and tactics to yourself— to your actions, habits, behaviors, associations, and style—to achieve the personal betterment and change you desire.

I am talking here not about just any kind of change, but about change that can make a lasting difference in your career and in your life. Think of shifting from one gear, from one way of being, to another. You can't flip-flop from program to program, from one resolution to another. True change springs from an idea whose time has come. It is powered by dissatisfaction with the way things are.

In other words, Shift is a change that lets you see yourself in a new light. Applying Shift to your life and career requires knowing what to keep, what to shed, and what to completely transform. Shift occurs when you assign ideas and values new priority. It will affect how you see others, and how others see you.

I've eaten oranges ever since my boyhood in Brooklyn. But when I decided to Shift my life once and for all, I started eating a lot more oranges. I started looking to oranges to transform my life. Do you want to transform your life? Be more successful? Make more money? Lose weight? Change your career or purpose? Then look for your own "oranges." Find something you can touch, something you can feel. Something you can stare at for a thoughtful moment when you need to reconnect with your sense of purpose and your sense of mission—with your sense of wanting to Shift.

The "orange" can be anything you want it to be. For my daughter, it was a new tattoo—a symbol of spiritual power to her. Looking at it centers her. My sister-in-law had a tough fight against breast cancer. The orange in her life was a piece of quartz dangling from a bracelet she wears every day. Sometimes even without thinking about it, she reaches down and touches the familiar rough quartz against her fingertips. And that touching—that physical contact—has a calming effect. It's all about finding what works for you. It's all about having a vision of Shift and sticking with that vision. That is what I did when I finally decided to change my life—the way I've changed scores of brands and products and companies in my professional career—and lose hundreds of pounds and give myself a completely different look.

Why Not?

THINK . . .

You have a plane trip in the morning: traveling for business from New York to Los Angeles. You work late to get everything ready. Your presentation is perfect. The potential of your trip is astounding. You can taste success. You pick up some Chinese take-out food and head home to pack. You eat from the health menu—steamed vegetables and chicken right from the container, with chopsticks. You have a cup of oolong tea, and at the end of your meal, feeling good, you open the fortune cookie. "Tomorrow is not a good day to travel," warns the fortune. Do you go on your trip anyway? Would you fly or would you cancel? If you got on the plane regardless of the prediction, would you be worried? Would you do something to counteract fate—say a prayer or wear a good luck charm?

If you cancel your trip because of the fortune cookie, it is fair to say that you believe that the future can be predicted and, in fact, already exists. If you disregard the fortune cookie's importance, it is fair to say that you believe that the future is what you make it, that you are responsible for your future. Today, I am the person who would eat the cookie, throw the fortune away, get on the plane, and do the job. And that was not always true of me. Today, I am the person who does not look for excuses or make them. I am not a victim of myself anymore. I also am not a doctor, a therapist, a preacher, or a self-help guru. I am a guy who did something that worked, and worked so well that I knew it would be irresponsible of me not to share how I achieved such success. I lost 256 pounds and gained a new life.

It sometimes scares people to hear someone talk about wanting more out of life. They hear a challenge or a rebuke to the way they've been living for years. But they are missing the point. I'm talking about how the present can be the lever to a new future. I'm talking about the power of change. Anyone who does what I do for a living comes away with a healthy respect for the potential of even a single minute—a minute spent watching a good TV commercial. Most people my age remember the first time they saw the classic Apple ad in 1984 that features a woman with a sledgehammer being chased by marching minions. Was that message, that impression, that indelible memory "only advertising"? Or how about basketball legend Charles Barkley declaring, "I am not a role model." Was *that* "only advertising"?

I want to challenge assumptions. And if you are up for that challenge, this book is for you. If you're willing to be surprised, to be astonished by the power of change, then stay with this thought: It's not your fault, whatever it is you think you've done or not done. You don't have to blame yourself. In fact, I insist that you don't—self-blame serves no purpose, believe me (I failed with my own diet many times before finding success). And once you accept that you don't have to blame yourself, you can open yourself up to something thrillingly new—or maybe to something old that you have the power to make new again.

Like a lot of people who work very hard and put in a lot of hours at the office, I see my work life as an extension of my private life. I don't make a neat distinction between them. I believe it's a terrible mistake to try to separate our professional lives from our own lives. This is not the era of the company man or company woman and no one has to pretend to check his or her personal life at the door and give everything to a corporate culture that demands adherence to business rules that fly in the face of personal values and needs. If you work in a corporate culture that in one way or another implies or tells you that a good "professional" always has a finger ready to lick and hold up to see which way the wind is blowing, at any expense to your personal happiness or fulfillment, it might be time for you to focus some of that energy back on yourself and on what will make you happy. It's time to integrate and live one life. I used to look a lot different than I do now. I used to be physically imposing—that's a diplomatic way to say that I was obese. My obesity was what people noticed first when they met me. I've always loved food. I used to devour good food the way I devour life, savoring every new sensation (or new thought) that comes to me over the course of the day. I still do that in my life, but not with food anymore. Eventually, my love affair with food made me seriously overweight.

Even as I kept eating and adding pounds, in my heart I wanted to slim down. I tried diets. I tried exercise. I tried meditation. I asked people for help. I asked my dogs for help. Nothing worked. When I weighed more than 400 pounds, I was limited to wearing a loose, billowing shirt and huge baggy trousers, day after day. My clothing sizes were off the charts. My neck was 19.5 inches, my waist size was 68 inches, and my jacket was a 56—then each piece was further let out by tailors to make them even bigger. My outfit never varied. That became my look, my brand. I could sense how prejudiced against me some people were because of my weight. Those people, who didn't know me, judged the book by its cover and assumed I was lazy or weak. Some felt sad for me. Others saw me as an unfit man who couldn't buckle his seat belt on a plane without an extender. But many times, they couldn't see *me* for myself. My girth didn't allow them to see beyond the surface.

Malcolm Gladwell, the *New Yorker* writer, makes a similar point about how people perceive us in his book *Blink: The Power of Thinking Without Thinking*, when he talks about the "weird power of first impressions." His motivation for writing the book, he explains, came from a personal event. The son of a black mother and a white father, Gladwell had decided to let his curly hair grow out, simply because he felt like it. Then something happened to him on the streets of New York that he believes would never have happened if his hair had been short.

The acclaimed, best-selling author and intellectual was stopped by three policemen, who said that they were looking for a rapist and Gladwell fit the description. They began to question him. Shown a sketch of the suspected rapist by the police, Gladwell saw that the only thing he had in common with the man was a big head of curly hair. After twenty minutes, the police let him go, but the experience burned on inside of Gladwell. This searing experience highlighted for him the way a first impression can define and stereotype in an instant who you are.

Stereotyping can work for you or against you. It is important to understand this as you work to brand or rebrand who you are and how you are perceived. And although branding yourself is a very personal act, in the end it is intended as a gift you give to others, who will make your brand their own. Once defined and out in the world, your brand will be taken on by others, from friends and family to coworkers and strangers who see you on the street. They will have an opinion about who you are to them.

I was on my way to finding all of this out for myself when I made the decision to remove the barriers to change I had created for myself, when I freed myself to go from more than 400 pounds to around 150. I decided to stop blaming myself for past mistakes and take possession of today so that I could lose the weight. I know now that removing barriers is the first act in setting yourself free. But I discovered that it's a long act; it can take your whole life, because as you eliminate one set of barriers, you will see others that you'll want to change. This is the nature of Shift, slight movements as made by the turtle, who knew that slow and steady wins the race.

I'm not comfortable telling you about the days when I weighed 406 pounds—I'd rather not—but it is necessary and part of paying change forward. Only when I decided to tap the power of what I had learned in my creative work about branding—about powerfully defining an idea and an emotional frame of reference—did I have the power to see my life in a new context and create a new set of realities about what was possible and not possible for me. It took me twenty years, constantly struggling with weight gain and weight loss, to finally click in to the idea that I, too, could benefit from some of my own branding and innovation expertise. I don't believe I was simply slow to apply myself to myself. I think the thought came, as most inspirations do, attached to some higher purpose that was no longer merely my own.

It's so funny, because we know these things when we are children. As children, enveloped in the golden light of curiosity, we embrace life without question or prejudice. But as adults, we are weighed down by our histories and past narratives. That baggage limits our ability to be open, to be truly and honestly alive, and to see things with the freshness that once came so naturally.

My goal in my work, in my life, and in this book is to get that freshness back. Achieving this is a path that will become a journey for life. Often my job can be explained as simply holding up a mirror to the inner truth of a product's or a company's identity. Truth is a difficult thing for us. We build mirrors in our lives that we think are reflections of our souls, but usually they are nothing more than distortions. The real trick is to devise a new mirror, one that can enable us to liberate our inner truth. Such optics can be painful, however—the truth is not always easy. You have to be able to face the truth head-on, without flinching.

Ralph Lauren once said, "I don't design clothes, I design dreams." Ralph, metaphorically of course, gives everyone who wears his clothes an Ivy League degree and a blue-blood heritage. When you go into his stores, antiques dominate the setting and look as though they were brought in from an English manor house. Ralph's vision goes beyond the necktie he began his empire with. Too often business leaders see their vision as something to be protected and doled out a little at a time. Plans are exposed in a series of quarterly meetings, each plan designed to be more exciting than the previous one. Too often business leaders try to solve for the limitations of an organization, instead of using that rusty metal can-opener to pry the old model apart and create an organization based on open-ended possibility—on what could and should be, not on what is. Many organizations talk about being truly integrated and not vertically driven, but more often than not, the environment needed to let this horizontal style flourish is not developed. When people in an organization are empowered to embrace their own vision, and to make contributions that transcend their narrowly defined responsibilities and duties, they tend to soar.

But we haven't yet learned how to liberate our minds.

Most people want to go to the party but feel they don't have an invitation. They feel that to be invited they have to get on the list. But the list, of course, is really nothing more than preconceptions and false beliefs. You just have to put your name on the list and you are there. My hope is that reading this book will enable you to design your invitation to your own fantasy, your own dreams, your own goals and passions.

After Robert F. Kennedy was assassinated, his brother Ted delivered a powerful and poetic eulogy. He finished with a quotation that both John and Bobby Kennedy had used, adapted from a line in a George Bernard Shaw play: "Some men see things as they are and say 'Why?' I dream of things that never were and say 'Why not?'"

Why not? Believing "why not" is a way of life. If you want to crack open a sense of possibility in your life and work, you're going to have a lot more luck if you show a willingness—a serious commitment—to "why not." Don't limit yourself or allow yourself to get stuck in the boxes others build for you. Don't compartmentalize your life. If you want to feel a wide-open sense of possibility, you need to knock down the walls and open up your life into one giant space, encompassing work and home life and everything else. I call this space "One Life." I think you'll find that the sky is *not* the limit, nor is the universe.

CHAPTER 3

The Art of Branding

I'VE BEEN CALLED a master of the art of visual branding and design language development. I helped reshape the images and messages of Reebok, Donna Karan, Samsung, GNC, ConEdison, and Pepsi, and I designed the Peapod, Chrysler's iPod-operated electric vehicle. But to be honest, I'm not at all excited by the notion of branding itself. What I'm excited about is how we can use branding as a tool to invent and design, create and re-create products, companies, and ourselves. I'm excited about what branding can do to shape and influence people. It can leave us permanently changed and strengthened, because branding at heart is about making connections and associations with people and things. It allows one to travel to other worlds, to discover new things, and in turn to be discovered. It is an ongoing journey that can make you more self-aware, and less likely to be misinterpreted by others. I am thrilled by marketing that is beautiful and powerful and eloquent. But with successful marketing, one needs to be able to see through branding as well, like a clear stream of water, to perceive the power of the message underneath.

So far as anyone has been able to work out, the first people to use hot metal to brand their animals as a form of identification were the ancient Egyptians, who often let their cattle feed in open fields. As early as 4,600 years ago, they used small marks, such as etchings on the horns, to mark their cattle. The practice continued over the years wherever people owned cattle or other livestock, and after European discovery of the "New World," the practice migrated across the Atlantic. Today the word *branding* is associated with value perception, image, big business, and intellectual property of all kinds. But originally branding was just an organizing principle.

Branding is also about ownership. In the past, Romans claimed ownership of a slave or livestock with an identity mark. Today, we as consumers see ourselves "owning" a piece of a company or a product's identity when we buy or associate ourselves with a specific brand or logo. Today, branding is a way of establishing who we are. It allows us to be part of something larger than ourselves in the same way that, hundreds of years ago, the Irish and the English and the French identified themselves through their emblems and crests.

The hidden emotional truth behind the reach and impact of branding is that people want to belong to something larger than themselves. We love to join Apple, and we do so by buying Apple products. We want to join the iPod, iPhone, or iPad club. We love to join "in" brands. The fundamental act of harnessing and capturing value in products, through building a community around products and helping to drive desire, is the centerpiece of modern-day marketing. We live in a society where people buy the dreams and identities they want. They long to fulfill those dreams, to feel replenished and revived. That is why Hollywood is so important. Music and films boil the blood and rush us toward destinations of dreams and aspirations. We need them like oxygen to survive. They are there for you, reminding that you can be your own aspiration, if you take the step. If you Shift. We yearn to create interesting, compelling new identities for ourselves. And successful marketers help to give them to us. The products or goods themselves are only an expression of that desire. It is advertising that encourages us to lean into our desires.

CHAPTER 4

Find Your Message

ONE WAY COMPANIES REACH consumers with their messages is by partnering with a popular figure, the way Ronald Reagan posed for print ads with Chesterfield cigarettes in the early 1950s. The biggest corporations line up celebrities to help create their brands. We believe in the credibility of a Michael Jordan or a Muhammad Ali for the right product—we know both athletes struggled and achieved something special with their talents and hard work. And we think we can be like them if we simply drink the same beverage or wear the same underwear.

In the early days of television advertising, Colgate, as the first toothpaste, just had to announce its existence and customers came running. What does a company do when a dozen different toothpastes are available? Or a hundred? More important, as consumers, how do we make a choice when given so many options?

Does choice come down to price? Shelf position? What about giving consumers confidence cues?

Well, these confidence cues come from advertising and marketing.

The ultimate act of branding is to take something—a product or service—and make everyone aware of it, and its purpose or intent. When you hear a baby cry, most people's first thought is that the baby is hungry—it needs milk. *Cry* equals *milk*. That is the kind of simplicity, the kind of instant connection, I strive for in branding.

You have to find the inner truth about the message of your product. To gain the loyalty and trust of consumers, your message—conveyed through advertising or marketing—has to be authentic. It has to be simple and boiled down to its essence. This is especially important in a marketplace where dozens of different brands for the same product are competing for attention.

Finding your inner truth is important in any personal efforts to change. To develop the new "you" that you have in mind, you have to build it around who you genuinely are. You have to strip the old facade away, with a big file or coarse sandpaper.

That's what we did in our ads for Rockport. They're the most comfortable shoes in the world, right? So I took a picture of a guy with his hands wrapped around a woman's bare foot, rubbing it gently. I didn't need to say anything more. Wearing the shoe feels as good as a foot massage. So why not just show a foot being massaged? You don't even have to show a shoe.

When you ask most people where electricity comes from, they will tell you it comes from the outlet in the wall. And in terms of their day-to-day experiences, they are right. So that became the inspiration for the communications program we created for ConEdison, New York's number-one utility company, as deregulation swept the industry.

In a deregulated market, New Yorkers would be faced with numerous new energy services companies, and ConEdison wanted to reassure its customers that the company would still be there to deliver their energy. ConEdison needed to define and differentiate its brand. We began by designing a new logo, a stylized depication of a socket and plug that got to the essence of what symbolized "energy" or "power" to most consumers. We applied this new logo to ConEdison hats, uniforms, trucks, and all communications, from letterhead stationery and consumer materials to Web sites. Next, we began to work on a communications program to define the brand's image and promise.

We came up with the tagline "On It." The beauty of "On It" is that it never overinflates expectation or promise. Often the key to success in getting your message across is having the quiet confidence to avoid over-promising to people—in other words, not unrealistically bragging but being honest, straightforward, and open with your audience. "On It" is not grandiose. The taglines of other energy companies expressed sentiments such as "Making sure your lights will never go out" and "Powering your life." But what happens when the electricity goes out in your neighborhood? The tagline becomes a Jay Leno joke. And worse, it becomes a lie. "On It" is always true. It is an honest, accurate statement about the company and how it delivers, responds, and operates. To reinforce the truth behind this, we featured the men and women of ConEdison in our communications, the workers whom New Yorkers see on the streets and in their buildings every day. I went into manholes, up poles, in cherry lifts, in the office, and on the street to capture them in action. During the shoot, a worker wearing a thick work glove gave me a thumbs-up, which I photographed and turned into the iconic image of the brand and the "On It" attitude.

I felt ConEdison energy needed to be seen as more than a plug or a switch. The company needed to be seen as a group of dedicated experts striving every day to keep things working—as people who are "On It." The campaign became an authentic representation of ConEdison and, by being true and honest to itself, generated well-deserved pride both among ConEdison workers and among New Yorkers.

When you redefine the essence of a brand, you have to stick with the brand's or the company's core values. When The Gap, headed by the legendary fashion brand marketer Mickey Drexler, bought Banana Republic in 1983, Banana Republic was a chain of safari stores. Giant plaster trees were "planted" in the center of the stores. Old Jeeps were used as displays. Safari, wilderness, and camping props were scattered throughout each store. The fishing vest that was on sale really was for fishing.

Mickey wanted us to rebrand Banana Republic as a store selling relaxed, tailored clothes for young men and women for work and casual wear. He intended Banana Republic to morph from a safari outfitter to an urban clothing brand. The decor was going to be clean, modern, and open. Customers would not have to walk around a makeshift campsite to get to a rack of shirts.

One of the first questions we asked Mickey had to do with the name of the store. Surely the first thing that had to go in order to shed the safari style was the name "Banana Republic."

His answer? Absolutely not.

The chain was well known to consumers; it had good name recognition, was associated with quality, and stood for adventure. Those are great values, Mickey pointed out. Our job was to translate those values into the new concept for the store. Over the next several years, we redefined what *adventure* meant at Banana Republic. It no longer meant venturing into the woods and pitching a tent. Instead, it meant trying something new, taking a walk in the park, crossing the street to see something special, or taking a new route to work. The adventure became more urban, more of an everyday life adventure.

We refined the logo to give it more elegance, creating a ℛ mark that looked like a monogram—something you would find on fine linens or designer clothing. We used design to help direct consumers to see the brand in a new way, without losing the Banana Republic name and the value it brought. We also designed a line of men's and women's fragrances and a collection of bath and body products. This was as much a strategic decision as it was about creating new product for the stores. A brand that has a luxury bath and body line and fine perfumes and colognes would no longer be associated with camping in the woods or jungle. Through focused advertising, graphic design, and product development, we worked with Mickey to maintain the core values of Banana Republic as he and his team created whole new collections, season after season, to help the spirit and adventure of the brand come alive in a whole new way.

I believe that the images used to brand products have to present universally familiar things in a way never seen before. Samsung, for example, wanted to sell microwave ovens to college students and young adults. So I took a guy with impressive six-pack abs and a rippling chest and put him, bare-chested, in jeans. I cut off the picture at the head and had him, with a little prop magic, hold the Samsung microwave under his arm. The image was both eye-catching and intriguing. The key idea we wanted to bring to life is that people wear their products, not just use them. Products are a lifestyle badge that transcends transaction. That's why brands are so meaningful. This was not some regular-looking guy. He was fit and in shape. He is the guy college guys wish they could be. Nothing else needed to be said. And the caption I wrote said exactly that: "Simply Samsung." If you show a kid carrying a microwave into a college dormitory common room, that's not an ad—or at least not a *good* ad. But if you show a fit, shirtless guy holding a Samsung microwave under his arm, everyone you reach will get the notion that a Samsung microwave is lightweight, compact—and sexy. And that maybe, since the guy holding the microwave looks so good, it is possible to eat healthy using a microwave oven. I believe this kind of aspirational currency is key to branding yourself, as much as it is to branding a product.

Branding is all about simplicity and scale. We tend to get excited over very, very basic things. Most people don't relate to small; they relate to big. So as a marketer, it pays to think really big and to move fast. You have to approach marketing like Formula 1 racing: respond quickly, think ahead, and know where you are going. Cassius Clay became Muhammad Ali by proclaiming, "I am the greatest." Before his fight with heavyweight champion Sonny Liston in February 1964, Ali was known as Cassius Clay. Before the fight, he composed a poem, which he called "I am the greatest":

This is the legend of Cassius Clay,
The most beautiful fighter in the world today. . . .
Yes, I'm the man this poem is about
I'll be Champ of the World, There isn't a doubt. . . .
I am the greatest!

He won the fight and the next day announced he would from then on be known by his new name, Muhammad Ali. He literally remade himself in a way no other sports figure ever has. He didn't claim to be the smartest. People would have argued with him about that. He said he was "the greatest." What could anyone say to refute that? Over time, we treated him as if he were the greatest.

CHAPTER 5

Brand "You"

THE SUCCESS of a brand is tenuous. Another product is always out there or ready to emerge to undercut or overtake yours, one that will brand your product negatively or promise more, take your market, steal your share, and try to kill you off. The same dynamic shapes your career. No matter what you have accomplished, always waiting in the wings are newcomers who have more interest in their own success than in the collective success of the team or company. There are even those who want to overtake you, knock you down, and get you out of the way.

The strongest branding backs everything into the product—in the design, marketing, experience, and communication, both virtually and physically. My philosophy is to make the product so robust in appearance, attitude, personality, and spirit that the competition can't copy it. That's how

Apple and Nike have carved out their own territory. They have spent time and resources building their identity, personality, values, and style into every one of their products. Apple's logo and Nike's Swoosh are critical tools to protect and *extend* their brands, not just sell their brands.

Historical figures such as Jesus Christ and Julius Caesar have been identified as brands—whether or not the word *brand* has ever been applied to them—as have fictional characters on classic TV shows such as *Gilligan's Island*: the professor in his white shirt and khaki pants; the trademark facial expressions and gestures of the skipper, going after Gilligan; the trademark utterances of the millionaire talking to his wife, "Oh, lovey!" The writers and producers and directors of such TV shows were showing in dramatized form what we all need to do to carve out a place for ourselves in today's fast-moving, all-involving media landscape, where news and human interest fold together on the Internet thanks to Facebook, YouTube, and Twitter. We all need to be the stars in our own dramatic movies. Today, people brands are some of the most powerful brands anywhere: Think of Oprah, Martha Stewart, Lady Gaga, and Will.i.am.

To rebrand yourself as an individual, the first thing you have to do is take all the values and history and uniqueness that are you and back them into the image you want to establish for your friends, colleagues, and the outside world. Too much is at stake to attempt this in a half-assed or scattered way. People think that if they get a five-hundred-dollar haircut or a two-thousand-dollar dress or suit, they'll look fabulous—confident, glamorous, successful—not realizing that no one will notice the suit or haircut if they are over-weight and out of shape.

To rebrand yourself, to make a major change in your career or your life, start by distilling who you are down to its essence. What do you want to communicate to others? What do you drive? Who do you hang out with? Where do you live? What do you read? How do you dress and behave? The answers to all of these reflect choices that help to form the brand that is you. This could be your chance of a lifetime to become one in a million.

When you define your brand and begin to establish a new and better you, you might have to be a grump, a tyrant, a bitch, or all of the above for a little while. Good-intentioned friends who think you deserve a "treat" are your new brand's worst enemy. They mean well, but veering from your chosen path will not be productive. You will need to be selfish, self-serving, self-absorbed, self-centric, and any other hyphenated *self* word you can think of to keep your focus and keep on track. A brand that acts this way is recognized and applauded as consistent, strategic, well-managed, and focused on what it stands for in the minds and hearts of its audience.

I believe an individual's brand today is increasingly important. It quickly communicates who we are. Consciously or unconsciously, we offer subtle cues to those around us. So why not do it consciously, with intent?

No matter where I go, personal struggle is everywhere and people want to talk about theirs—how they have it in their lives, how they are dealing with it, and, if they were lucky, how they overcame it. These conversations can range in topic from the devastating earthquake in Haiti in early 2010 to an illness to just bad luck. Conversations about personal struggle connect people more deeply and profoundly than nationality, race, religion, or world events. No matter where I am, if I tell people that I lost 256 pounds, they have a story for me, a great, personal story from which I always learn something new.

I recently met a man named Sergio. He was our driver/tour guide. When we got into his car for the ride from the airport in Naples to our hotel, he hooked a microphone around his neck and began to talk, giving a mini tour. We were in a small van, and a microphone was not at all a necessity. I asked Sergio why he was using one. What he said is one of the smartest, most well-stated personal branding strategies I have ever heard: "You can only win by having the lowest price or by giving the most value. I won't lower my price so I have to give more value." Hence the differentiated and superior experience of a professionally "broadcast" tour. Sergio was smart enough not to lower his price and savvy enough to take his personal brand to the next level.

CHAPTER 6

The Secret Behind Shift

TOO OFTEN, the effort to make a radical, sudden change in your life turns out to be unsustainable. I believe it is better to keep in mind the famous marketing phrase "New and improved!" My goal from the beginning in losing weight was to find a "New and improved!" version of Peter Arnell, to uncover a different version of myself. Drastic change was the enemy, never the goal. Think about your future self as the brand as you always have been, only a better version. Work with people in your life to help yourself unlock that better self—the same but improved you. Do not set out to transform yourself into a completely new brand. In the end, if you change enough, others will come to see you in a new way. After all, change is in the eye of the beholder.

The story of me and my weight loss is only one example of how to make a Shift in your life. But it's a useful one, since weight loss or control is something that many people wrestle with at one point or another. I am not a man who likes to exercise. It wasn't me to try to go to the gym regularly to work out. Nor was I ever going to become a yoga enthusiast or a marathon runner—no way, no how. But I knew I didn't need to change who I was so radically. All I needed, it was clear to me, was to set in motion the levers of Shift. They are the same levers that you can set in motion in your own life, no matter what aspect of yourself you want to change.

I rarely exercised while I was trying to lose weight. And when I did exercise, it was not in order to lose weight but for cardiovascular benefits. This was not necessarily the right choice or the healthiest—I am not proud of my aversion to exercise. But I knew I needed to be true to myself. Because I had rarely exercised, I did not want to commit to this activity that I didn't enjoy and, I knew instinctively, would not be able to keep up. It would have been too big a change for me.

Surgery was never an option for me either. Surgery would have been the opposite of Shift. It would have been too extreme a change, a shock to my system, one that would have disrupted everything I had been working to build. I was afraid such a radical approach would lead to my putting the weight back on. I wanted weight loss that I myself achieved, not something abruptly engineered from without. My doctor, Louis Aronne, a nationally recognized expert on obesity, explained that weight loss is a matter of simple math, and that I could make this math work for me. I needed to keep in check the proportion of calories taken in versus calories burned, and nature would take care of itself. And he was right. Losing weight was almost that simple, although I needed to stick with foods that had a low glycemic index so I could keep my insulin levels regulated. I decided to focus on my calorie intake and be single-minded about reducing it and keeping it low.

Losing weight without surgery enabled me to shift my eating habits instead of changing who I was. The human body is a machine. It took about two weeks of discipline to get my body working for me, not against me. A lot of people who quit smoking say later that the first two weeks are the hardest. It was the same for me in stopping my unhealthy eating habits. Those two weeks were a real trial. I had to strain to resist urges, break old habits, and live a life that was both the same yet different. Keeping track of what I ate was critical. I used to count out thirteen cashews for a snack. Not twelve cashews, not fourteen, but *thirteen*! Once I counted them out, that was exactly how many I ate, no exceptions.

Dr. Aronne designated what he called "unlimited" foods for me, such as salad and green vegetables. I could eat as much of them as I liked. So I meticulously counted any foods that were on the "Limited" list and ate freely from the "unlimited" list. This gave me a mental break from having to think constantly about every single morsel of food I was putting in my mouth and how many calories it represented. I had a technique to get my mind *off* the diet, which was as important as keeping my mind *on* the diet.

I also drank a lot of water—about eight 32-ounce bottles of Fiji water a day. Drinking water did two important things: It kept my hand-to-mouth urges constantly occupied, and it helped me to feel clean and flushed out. It was a healthy and proactive way to keep my diet at the top of my mind. Drinking so much water kept my stomach full, which helped stem hunger pangs, but drinking all that water was not just about food. It was about taking care of my entire body. It even helped keep my skin healthy and hydrated, so that I never had that waxy-looking skin you see on some people who have lost a lot of weight. Drinking water became a ritual, a routine, a rerouting of my impulses, and it led to a healthier me.

I still dined out at my favorite restaurants. I worked with the managers and chefs and owners to tailor my meals to how I needed to eat in order to lose weight. And that was important. It's important not to eliminate things that make you happy. I love going out to eat, to socialize and for my work. You need to find ways to be happy within your routines and lifestyle. This is what Shift is all about. I was able to be happy with a delicious grilled chicken salad at Da Silvano, and with sushi wrapped in cucumber, without rice, at Nobu or Hatsuhana, instead of pasta and tempura. The experience was the same—the same location, the same people, the same routine—so it became easy to eat differently. I was changing only one thing—what I ate—not my entire way of being.

Weight loss always starts with a decision. I didn't need an *in*-cision. You have to make a *de*-cision to change your life. It all starts with the mind. I needed to develop greater discipline and more willpower than I had before. I needed to feel compassion for my family and for others close to me who were, in a way, embarking with me on this demanding trip. Their journey, however, was involuntary.

The first step toward strengthening my mind was to see myself as a fat person. Any mirror could show me that I was a 400-pounder. But I didn't see myself that way. I saw myself as a creative person, and that self-image canceled out everything else, leaving no room in my imagination to see myself as a chubby person or even as a person on a diet. So I needed to give myself a reality check. And my family needed to give me a reality check as well. The people who love you the most are sometimes the ones least equipped to help you. My kids never said anything to me about being fat. They didn't want to hurt my feelings, so they told me I looked great. They said they loved my style. But elastic-waisted pants and untucked white shirts are not a "style" or a fashion statement.

So step one toward Shift was to stop kidding myself, to give my family and closest friends permission to be honest with me. That honesty hurt my feelings a little, but it was a good kind of hurt. It was like an ice cold splash of water to the face to help get me—and keep me—on track.

Change is a two-way process. It is important that any change you achieve be recognized as much by other people as by yourself. The process is complete only when people say about you, "He really changed his life!" or "She is a completely new person!" or "He is so much calmer than before!" That is the real sign of success. That's when you know you have Shifted to a new way of being. That's when you know that the change you made is here to stay. That's why encouraging acknowledgment is so important, so critical to change. The two-way confirmation is what makes it all come true.

Change comes true when people notice it. That is what I learned on my way from 400-plus pounds to 150 pounds. And that is what I want to help you discover for yourself.

CHAPTER 7

Fish Where the Fish Are

TO SUCCESSFULLY REACH other people through branding, and to zero in on the emotional truth of your subject, you have to draw inspiration and perspective from your own life. I'm not saying you need to be a saint or a sage. As much as I'd love to have the Dalai Lama on my team, I'm aware that His Holiness is otherwise engaged. But if we are blind to our inner selves, we can never learn the important lessons that we have all experienced and felt. And if we can't use that experience in our work and our lives, we will always be robbing ourselves of the potential to soar in whatever we are doing. That is the core message of this chapter. Our memories are fickle and fallible. But that's all the more reason to treat them with respect and care, to view them as the emotional warehouse they are, not as an enemy or an obstacle to be overcome.

My earliest memory is painfully clear, like some snippet

of a lost and forgotten 8 mm film jerking all over the screen in front of an old Super 8 projector. In the film, something terrible has happened, but at first I don't know what. I just know that people seem startled, stunned, jolted from whatever they were doing five minutes earlier. It is a November afternoon, a Friday, in Brooklyn in the 1960s. I'm staying with my grandparents, who recently moved into a big apartment building built shortly before the start of World War II, on Shore Boulevard right at the end of Sheepshead Bay.

I am in a nearby park playing with my friends as my babysitter, Ethel, keeps an eye on us. I look up and see my grandmother rushing across the street toward me. Just the sight of her out on the street in her yellow paisley housedress, white handkerchief in hand, is enough to startle me. Then I notice that she is crying, which really throws me for a loop. It's unnerving to see this proper English woman losing her grip when she has always been so in control. She grabs my hand so hard it scares me for a minute. Looking up into her face, I see her reddish eyes, tears rolling down her cheeks.

My grandmother pulls me across the street, and we hurry back to the apartment building, up the big brick front steps, through the wide double doors facing out toward Sheepshead Bay, and into the lobby, as if we are on some kind of mission. Along the way, we run into a few of the neighbors. They are crying, too, and no one seems to know what to say.

Back up in the apartment, I think maybe my grandmother will calm down and life will go back to normal. Instead, she walks me over to my toy chest, my vast treasure trove of playthings.

"Peter, I want you to throw away all your toy guns!" my grandmother tells me.

I love my toy guns. Why does she want me to got rid of them? None of this makes any sense. To me the toys represented happiness, endless hours of playing G.I. Joe, soldiers and horses, cowboys and Indians. Bang, bang, you're dead! But she is serious. With a heavy heart, I gather my toy soldiers and pop guns and cap guns and military rifles and hand them to my grandmother. She takes them all, and we walk downstairs to the incinerator. I feel sad. Tears were streaming down my face. What have I done wrong?

"Guns kill people," my grandmother says after throwing the last of the toy guns into the incinerator. "Our president was killed today by a gun."

November 22, 1963, was a terrible moment in U.S. history, the day President John F. Kennedy was killed. I was far too young to understand that at the time. The searing pain of that day was too intense for me to grasp with anything like clarity and too personal for me to connect with the pain of other people. That's what it's like for a child, when emotions are too powerful to handle. All we can do as children is hold on to them and hope that later, eventually, we might gain the tools to make some sense of them. It's no exaggeration to say that to this day I can feel the pain from my memories of that afternoon.

The lesson I learned from that day—about the importance of drawing on the past, even when doing so hurts—was easily worth the agony and confusion and numbness I was hit with. Most of us probably don't think enough about the importance of appreciating the past and respecting its power to give us the means to learn new lessons, painful as well as pleasant ones. When we are evaluating the world around us, and deciding who we want to be, it's vitally important to draw on both our positive and our negative experiences, on the insights we glean from the things we see and touch, from the people we meet, and, yes, from the books we've read.

In 1963, I did not have even a remote grasp of what it meant that John F. Kennedy had been shot and killed in Dallas. But the incomprehensible made its debut in my life that day in a way that was indelible and lasting. That trip to the incinerator has stayed with me, and to this day I can't bring myself to throw anything away. I'm a collector—of memories, of things, of people in my life. Collecting helps me to keep moments alive. It spurs memory. It is important to have triggers that allow you to think back as you move forward. Such triggers are like touchstones. I find it's good to keep grounded in the meaningful past as I stride into the unknown future. Doing so makes change seem more purposeful, more deliberate, and less haphazard and experimental. It's important for me to be true to who I am as I endeavor to change myself. I collect tons of things: dried leaves and twigs from a memorable autumn trip, bottle openers from places I love, paper napkins, photos, postcards—mementos that help me remember a place, a time, and a feeling. The purpose of collecting for me is "saving my life," literally and figuratively.

I want to underscore my message here: *Don't ignore the*

lessons from the past to help change who you are in the pres-
ent! Don't think the past is over! Nothing is ever over in life.
Most people learn to let go of things or actively cast them
away. I've found that I'm not good at that. I can't let go of
anything. Every day, I collect artifacts from wherever I am—
matchbooks and memories, things you'd think no one would
want to save. I think the way I hold on to things is a strength,
and I wish more people would hold on to things. Often, if you
don't feel ready to let go of something, you may have a good
reason, though you may not be able to recognize it at the time.
You sense there is still something important for you, even if
you're not smart enough or focused enough or brave enough
to know exactly what it is. That is why I hold on to so much.
I'm glad that I have a way of remembering all kinds of things.
They stay with me; I rethink them over and over, teasing out
the meaning, drawing out the lessons. Sometimes these wrin-
kles of time push me through to something new and wondrous
in my work that finds its way into a brand.

I constantly look back to my childhood for clues about how
to live. I'm sure many of us do this to some degree. The interesting thing is what we do with those clues. I remember
what it was like for me as a teenager in Sheepshead Bay to
ride into work with my grandfather during the summer. I went
to sleep early, then woke up before midnight to pile into my
grandfather's cream-and-butterscotch-colored Buick Skylark
for the ride to the Fulton Fish Market at the South Street Seaport. It was a thrill at that age, heading toward the gleaming

skyline of Manhattan, though the ride often lulled me back to sleep before we rolled over the Brooklyn Bridge. We pulled off at the first exit in Manhattan and parked in Grandpa's regular spot under the bridge.

My grandfather would yank open the driver's-side door of the Buick and that always woke me up. A boy of fourteen or fifteen or sixteen, still half asleep, I looked up at the Wall Street skyline and at the span of the bridge stretching back toward Brooklyn, murky and mysterious and majestic, shrouded in mist. It was the most beautiful view I've ever seen, and it is burned, engraved, onto my imagination.

Those trips from Brooklyn to Manhattan were all about boyhood yearning—to be bigger or better or faster. But they also were about my fear that my goals and hopes and dreams might never be reached. Norman Podhoretz, in his memoir, wrote, "One of the longest journeys in the world is the journey from Brooklyn to Manhattan—or at least from certain neighborhoods in Brooklyn to certain parts of Manhattan." Going over the bridge with Grandpa was a combination of a tease and a test, entering one of the world's greatest cities.

The real heyday of the South Street Seaport had been from the 1840s to the 1880s. For me, entering the market was like walking into living history, seeing the shadows of past waves of Italian immigrants, and feeling a direct connection with Alfred E. Smith's boyhood New York. The young Al Smith, later governor of New York and Democratic presidential candidate, quit school when his father died and went to work at the Fulton Fish Market.

By the 1970s the Fish Market had seen better days. But it was still bustling and packed with people—and fish, every type of fish you could imagine, from fat slippery eels to jaggy-finned sea sturgeon, from porcupine fish to triggerfish, from cod and sea bass to porgie and flounder. Their scales flew all over the place and piled up in the market's corners like drifting snow.

Grandpa specialized in freshwater fish, which were easier on the nose than saltwater species. The fish market stank in a way that hit you over the head long before you ever walked inside, and the odor didn't let go of you until long after you'd gone. For a kid like me, always looking around at everyone and everything with big, curious eyes, it was an amazing magical place. To the burly, grizzled men in overalls and rubber aprons who worked there, I was like a mascot; they all said hello to me, calling out with their chewed-down cigar butts wedged into the corners of their mouths as they swung big hooks at the fish they were working on. They rubbed the top of my head as if they wanted to see if my mop of unruly dark hair would rub right off. Most of the time they answered the questions I threw at them, which was generous of them, considering the number and variety of the questions I always had.

Grandpa had come over from Russia, the old country, like so many others. He had an old-country seriousness about him, especially when he shared his reflections about life, passing on nuggets of wisdom or experience. I loved it when he did so, because those were rare occurrences. Whenever I asked him something, his first response was always the same.

"Have you thought about it, Peter?" he invariably asked.

"Yes, Poppa," I'd reply. "Yes, I have."

"No, no, no, Peter," he'd say. "Have you *thought* about it?"

He would repeat the question over and over. And often, I realized that I hadn't actually thought about what I was asking. And often, I realized that I already knew the answer. But sometimes Grandpa shared a nugget of wisdom.

"If you sell them bad fish, they're not going to come back, Peter," he sometimes said in a serious tone of voice.

He meant: People have noses. If the fish smell bad, people are going to notice. If they bring the fish home and notice a bad smell, they are going to hold that against you. In life and in business, it's a warning I've always kept in mind. The ultimate impact of what you deliver will be based on the true qualities, of what you actually have to offer, not on what you might have been trying to offer or hoping to offer or expecting to offer. When a fish smells bad, there is no such thing as an excuse. A fish smells bad or it doesn't.

"Peter, fish where the fish are," my grandfather also said.

Simple words, but powerful and true. Yet many people ignore them. At first they sounded like a chant to be said over and over again. *Fish where the fish are.* But eventually I saw how much sense Grandpa's words made.

His words had the power to transform me from a little boy who had grown up in Brooklyn crazy about playing stickball and kickball and basketball into a man who came to insist on chasing down the highest-quality experiences, who tries to spend every hour of every day wondering how I can be truer and braver and more daring and more present with every brand I work on, with everything I do in my life.

Fish where the fish are. It's the way I try to act and think, the way I focus on a problem or idea or solution. If I'm fishing here and the fish are jumping there, then there is where I want to be. I'm not interested in fishing where I've been taught to fish or told to fish. I'm not interested in the ideas I've been told to be interested in. If I change direction suddenly, in mid-sentence or mid-thought, it's because I'm constantly fishing where the fish are, whether the fish are customers, ideas, better ways of doing things, or a pure view into what a product's true essence is. When the school of fish zigs, then *I* zig.

At the fish market with my grandfather, I figured out that we can all learn a lot from fish if we pay close attention. The fish know what they're doing. If we want to catch those fish, we need to think the way the fish do.

I'm always ready to dart this way or that way, to respond to changing circumstances. I think that to be successful, you have to be alert to changing situations, and be ready to move with the fish. Some people have trouble keeping up with all that motion, with the constant change. I sense their confusion when my brain is firing in all directions to solve a business or marketing problem. I will be talking about something when—*ping*—I'm off in a different direction. Some people are surprised by my sudden changes in direction. I see them asking themselves, *Why is he jumping around so much? Why is he suddenly shifting the direction of the conversation?* And the answer is, I'm going where the fish are.

People who work closely with me sometimes get tired of

hearing about fishing where the fish are. I get tired of hearing it myself. But I always come back to it, because you know what? It's true. It's the starting point of any real success. Life's short. You have to go right at it and go big, because people care about big ideas, not small ones. You have to be where the action is. To get ahead in life, you have to fish where the fish are.

CHAPTER 8

Branding and the Power of Positive Emotions

BRANDING IS PRIMARILY about creating emotion. The word *emotion* has roots in a latin verb that means to remove or displace something. It turns out that emotion and motion are more closely connected than we commonly think. The strictly rational part of our minds may remember the fact that *pi*—3.14159265 . . . —is a useful word in euclidean geometry, allowing us to calculate the circumference of a circle. But it is only a number. No sights, sounds, or smells—no feelings—are associated with it. Contrast this *pi* with *pie* of a different kind, such as a freshly baked apple pie just out of the oven, which likely evokes a series of emotional associations, as well as tastes and smells. For most of us, the word *pie* instantly conjures up a very particular, good feeling.

There is a reason why our reactions to *pi* and *pie* are

different. Our memories of each are stored in different parts of our brains. When thinking of either word, we activate circuits in distinctly different regions of the brain.

The part of my brain that can regurgitate the value of pi is the cerebral cortex, the impressively corrugated layer on top of the upper lobes. It's the thinking part of the brain that other animals don't have; it's what makes humans unique. The rumble in my stomach that occurs when I hear the word *pie* gets funneled through more primitive parts of the brain inherited from our ancestors. Collectively called the limbic system, these structures, including the all-important hypothalamus and amygdala, are where fear is registered and processed, and they serve as a kind of trip wire. Emotion can bypass the thinking part of the brain and travel straight to the hypothalamus, triggering reactions such as the fight-or-flight reflex, driving our pulse rate higher and giving us a burst of alertness and energy.

Fear and other strong emotions have a dramatic edge when it comes to getting people's attention. When people are afraid, their amygdalas and hypothalamuses work together to short-circuit the centers of rational thought and memory, consideration and contemplation. Logical arguments are displaced by loaded slogans.

Without question, fear can give companies a lever to move consumers. Fear is very effective, but it has its downsides, too. It has a way of cutting a wide swath and making everything associated with it scary or ugly. People who are repeatedly prodded through the use of fear eventually grow inured to the prodding or become disgusted and revolt. Eventually, they see through such a brand's manipulation. And when that happens, they become angry.

I prefer to target positive emotions in my work. I prefer to unlock a sense of wonder, to package an uplifting sense of fun. I strive to step back from narrow personal concerns and to impart a message that can give people hope. Positive emotions are powerful motivators and trump fear. A person who has been pointed in the direction of sunshine and light knows enough to keep out of the way of the long shadow looming in the distance.

I can't think of a better example of this than the work my agency did for SoBe Lifewater. The dancing lizards became the talk of the Super Bowl for two years. Sometimes you have to ask the audience to suspend disbelief, to do something so fantastical and unexpected that people get swept up in the moment and become believers. Think Peter Pan.

SoBe Lifewater is what those in the beverage industry call a functional water beverage. I stress the word *functional*. This great-tasting flavored water is enhanced with lots of vitamins, antioxidants, and herbs to provide advanced health benefits over ordinary tap water. And you might think that it needs to be advertised in a very straightforward, *explanatory* way with a TV spot or a magazine ad that mentions the natural fruit flavors, explains the benefits of all the vitamins and herbs for your mind and body, and describes how some flavors are naturally sweetened with a plant extract and have zero calories. That's what the competition does.

But when we began the SoBe campaign, I didn't want consumers to assume that one brand of vitamin-enhanced water is as good as another. I wanted to make sure consumers liked SoBe for what it is and what it stands for. So we took SoBe's lizard logo, the symbol of the brand, and brought it to life by designing lizard characters through high-tech CG animation with the genius artists at Digital Domain. We created a group of lizards in many colors, shapes, and sizes to represent all the brand's flavors and varieties. And we made them dance. The dancing SoBe lizards feel no less real than celebrity athletes who endorse other drinks. It seemed to me to be a natural fit, since lizards live in a pure, natural environment. They are also very cool. And it took a village to get this done. Without the work of Naomi Campbell; the music organization and talent of Quincy Jones, Michael Jackson, and Peter Lopez; the styling by André Leon Talley, who searched through racks of vintage clothing for days before finding the perfect Karl Lagerfeld dress; and extraordinary partnership with our client Massimo D'Amore; and on and on, we probably would have ended up with "good," not "great!" The point is, get help and get the best you can, be it a friend or a professional.

Next, we created a series of television ads in which Naomi and the lizards, when they drank SoBe Lifewater, immediately were refreshed and energized. We were able to showcase the product's benefits with entertainment and style. Does anyone really need a long-winded explanation of the benefits of enhanced water? The best way to get people to remember and believe your story is to get them to smile, to get them to leave their reality behind for a moment and join yours. We all need a little escape in our lives. Being whimsical and a little "crazy" now and then can be healthy and fun. So remember to find your "crazy." Remember to keep your brand fun along the way. Change is difficult. Adding some lighthearted escape for yourself and those who support you will go a long way toward helping them to keep believing.

CHAPTER 9

Overcoming Fear

THERE ARE TIMES when I feel lost and need to ground my-self in who I am. I imagine that's a feeling many people have from time to time. But we're unwilling to pry that fear or con-fusion open for all to see. So we try to ignore it or push it down, rather than embracing those moments of vertigo, those confusing but occasionally thrilling times when we can see life's possibilities in an entirely different light. At those re-markable moments, our internal compass shifts. To embrace change, however, we have to be able to break through that barrier of fear and push through to self-discovery.

What does pushing through that barrier of fear feel like? Think of *Batman,* the TV show from the 1960s with Cesar Romero as a vamping-it-up Joker and Adam West and Burt Ward wearing tights in campy versions of Batman and Robin.

When they fought, the camera cut away at the moment of impact, and the words *POW!* or *BAM!* or *ZOWIE!* appeared on the screen, in place of special effects. That's how it feels when you push past the barrier of fear and momentarily break free: You feel something decisively changing inside you; the change is so vivid and cinematic that it seems to require sound effects. In a way, I'm talking about an act of violence, an act of aggression that you commit against those parts of yourself that are holding you back. As an act, it has to be cutting and deep. And it has to be done without hesitation or introspection.

Such an act, I've found, can take you in exciting—and terrifying—directions. Once you break through the barriers, you start to encounter different versions of yourself, all competing to have their perspective carry the day. I recommend you give them a full hearing. Unleash them. Free these alternative, competing aspects of yourself to mill around and talk to each other. Give them space for a frank exchange. I do this all the time. I've discovered I am made up of many personalities, depending on the circumstances I'm in, and it's never dull or disappointing when I let them talk to one another.

I feel we don't spend enough time thinking about our multiple personalities or dimensions. Most of us are too afraid to own up to our multiple selves. I'm not talking about multiple personality disorder, as in the film *Sybil*. Unlike Sybil, I know about my different personalities and am happy to let them peacefully coexist. Sybil had no idea she had multiple personalities within her; they emerged in response to extreme psychological trauma.

Am I scaring you? Let me explain what I mean. People see us in many different ways. Sometimes people don't like what I have to say and therefore don't like me very much. They don't like my attitude, or, as I have been told, they think I come on too strong. Others see me as a guy with a huge heart and a mind that is always active, someone who is generous and sharing. The fact is, both perceptions of me are true, depending on the situation or the context.

Each of us is scared much of the time. Being scared is one of the central constraints in our lives and imaginations. We're afraid to reveal our fragility and our weaknesses. We refuse to do anything that would expose ourselves or make ourselves vulnerable. So we hide out, tucked in our shells, and keep our different personalities or selves under wraps. We prefer to describe our weaknesses with mere captions. The unarticulated or the unimagined is easier to live with. In fact, we consider such silence to be a virtue. We think of it as a mature way to act or respond—seeing ourselves as quiet, unflappable professionals or partners.

I have found the reverse to be true. When you provide yourself with the keys to unlock greater emotional truth, you experience life through a deeper palette of colors, and you gain a truer and more intoxicating sense of life and work and what it all means.

In rebranding companies and products (and in rebranding myself), I found it is important to learn what it's like to be a child again, to want to "pet the tiger." Didn't we all want to do that as kids? Pet the tiger in the zoo? We were fearless at that age. A child can happily run too fast through a bumpy sandbox, blissfully unaware of the laws of physics and gravity. A child may take a hard fall, cry, then do it all again a few minutes later, blissfully ignorant of the lessons to be learned later about what he or she cannot do.

A child sees a big, orange-and-black–striped cat with beautiful liquid eyes and gleaming fur in the zoo and wants to reach a hand in through the bars of the cage and pet it. That child is not stopped by fear that the tiger will bare its teeth and bite and does not worry that the tiger will unleash a blood-curdling snarl so frightening that it can literally paralyze a person with fear. That child is happy not to impose limits to his or her imagination and thereby turn off his or her desire out of concern for some possible consequence. That child simply wants to pet the tiger.

I believe that within every one of us there still lives a child who wants to stand, smiling, before the tiger and reach out to pet that beautiful, luxurious striped fur. Within each of us is an untethered, fearless soul waiting to be released. If we can set our minds and souls free, we can turn off some of the preprogrammed warnings and limitations—fears—we place on ourselves that all too often leave us in an intellectual straitjacket.

We spend so much time stuck on treadmills in our careers and in our lives. We find ourselves trapped by the fear that we will disappoint others or disgrace ourselves. Instead of prodding us to change, our fear limits our behavior and wears us down, guaranteeing we will keep plodding along, predictable and uninspired and uninspiring. The alternative—to remain always a child, a student of life—is scary, and possibly painful. But it is liberating. It is painful only because it is at odds with the norms of society and marks us as different, as "the other."

How can we regain a sense of childlike fearlessness? What can inspire or motivate us? Although we devour movies of inspiration and courage, sagas of warriors and gladiators, we somehow manage to keep their core message at an emotional distance. We think of them as "entertainment," instead of allowing them to feed our imaginations and souls, to inspire us to find courage and heroism within ourselves. We allow good movies to thrill or temporarily transport us, but we don't let them touch us. We have a hard time taking in something larger than our individual lives.

I think we need to reach out to others, to create partnerships, with objects, with thoughts, with history, with other people, with knowledge, with nature. We need to embrace the power of *we*. Life itself is a collaboration. And embracing this kind of collaboration, this kind of partnership, can lead to a form of paradise.

Paradise may seem an odd word here, but I think it's appropriate. The ancient Greeks used the word *paradeisos* to refer to an enclosed park, borrowing a word of Iranian origin, which migrated to Latin and eventually to Middle English as *paradis,* as in Chaucer's line in *Canterbury Tales:*

"Noon other life," said he, "is worth a bene!
For wedlock is so esy and so clene
That in this world it is a paradis."

One of the definitions of *paradise* that you'll find in *Merriam-Webster* is "a place or state of bliss, felicity, or delight." Okay, that's not bad, but it leaves much unsaid.

I believe paradise is a place where there is no fear. To reach paradise, you have to rid yourself of fear, because fear can be a horribly limiting emotion. The great things that have been accomplished did not happen as a result of fear; they took place because of what it took to drive fear away. Buddha sat under a tree for forty-nine days, refusing to move until he discovered the truth and became enlightened. At this point, he believed he found the cause of human suffering and the steps one needed to take to eliminate it. Any search for paradise takes discipline and focus.

Imagination and collaboration, I believe, can drive fear away. Knowledge, too, can banish fear.

In a world too often filled with destruction, I believe our obligation is to provide a safe haven for ourselves and for others, a place in which we no longer have to be afraid. *Paradise.* When you are liberated from fear, you gain energy and a focus that make anything possible. You are able to move past old limitations, to Shift contours of your life. You can use that concept of Shift to achieve even the most far-fetched of dreams—such as losing over half of your body weight.

CHAPTER 10

Lessons from History

I WAS NO WORLD TRAVELER as a kid. My idea of a long trip when I was growing up was taking the D train into Manhattan. I didn't even do *that* very often. Mostly I ran for the train early in the morning, a scared little kid going to school or to one of the many part-time jobs I had as soon as I was old enough to talk someone into paying me to do something. If I wanted to buy something, I had to earn the money myself. It was absurd and pointless to ask anyone in my family to give me even a nickel when I was growing up. We just didn't have it.

I had more jobs than I could count. At one point I worked at a school supply store early in the morning—I had to be on the Sheepshead Bay subway platform by quarter to six to catch the D train to make it to work on time. At night I washed dishes at Junior's, the famous New York City diner renowned for its cheesecake. At other times I worked at the

Mobil gas station at the corner of Neptune Avenue and Shore Boulevard, or at Waldbaum's supermarket bagging at checkout. On Saturday evening I worked at Shelley's Luncheonette, right around the corner from our apartment building, folding the different sections of the Sunday *New York Times* together to make those big, towering piles of fat Sunday papers that are such a part of Saturday evening in New York to this day.

I was, in other words, just like a lot of other kids who grew up in New York City over the years as the son or grandson of immigrants. That's what Brooklyn is all about, ethnicities blending and melding side by side and spilling over into the culture at large. There is less breathing space in Manhattan, where everyone is squeezed more tightly together. But Brooklyn has oxygen. To grow up in Brooklyn was to feel a sense of space without limits. You had a beautiful beach crowded with an incredible variety of people, the Atlantic Ocean stretching out in front of you. Europe was out there right beyond the horizon somewhere, you knew. In Manhattan people always seemed to be stressed out, but in Brooklyn they had time to dream.

I wouldn't change a thing. But I won't deny that I missed out on just being a kid, working all those jobs, so desperate to get ahead. At the time you're not aware that you're missing out on part of your childhood. The memory does come back in later years. But if you recall your childhood in the right way, the memory can help you. I have mined my past countless times to help me in my work and in my life. To a lot of people, a tough childhood is an education in the school of hard knocks. I take a different view—I see it as a school of *good* knocks, at least for anyone willing to do to the work of pulling the good part out of it. It's a great opportunity to come to understand yourself better, even if doing so sometimes takes time—perhaps many, many years.

As far back as I can remember, I always had a rich fantasy life and imagination. I could always see things in my mind very vividly. My imagination could never be contained by the old neighborhood. My imagination today as an adult owes everything to keeping alive what it felt like for me as a young boy running for the subway early in the morning, eager to grab hold of life.

But when I was barely out of my teens, my imagination had an early chance to go on vacation.

After studying architecture in college, I worked in the Princeton, New Jersey, office of architect Michael Graves. Graves decided to have me work with my roommate, Ted Bickford, to design and lay out a small exhibition catalog for the Galleria Nazionale d'Arte Moderna. I had to spend several months in Italy going back and forth, coordinating all. I was in completely over my head, which of course was the beauty of this experience. Suddenly I was in the midst of museum directors and film directors and graphic artists and furniture designers and architects and publishing people and famous artists, such as Leonardo and Michelangelo, Bernini, Boromini, and Caravaggio, who weren't even alive in the traditional sense (although they were very alive to me). Don't think you can't meet and be seduced by the vision of people who are no longer among the living.

I fell in love with Italy; it became a second home to me. To this day I never feel quite as at home as I do when I'm in Italy, thanks to my extreme good fortune in being embraced full-time by an entire family, whom I met early in my life and who adopted me as one of their own. They all had distinct, vivid identities. The head of the family, the patriarch, I thought of as the industrialist. One member of the family was a school-teacher; she took care of her students in the same way she took care of all of us. Another member of the family was the family philosopher, who did in fact end up becoming a pro-fessor of philosophy. Another was an architect, which made him doubly my brother. One was an artist. And the last, the youngest, was a free spirit, a filmmaker who worked in ad-vertising and marketing and commercials. He was later, trag-ically, killed in an avalanche. My Italian family became my home, my office, my everything.

I was young and scared and had to learn the importance of failing. No matter what you know, what you *don't* know al-ways remains more important in your journey and progress. If you remain in a constant search for what you *don't* know, the chances of your growing and learning are much greater. Yes, that's at odds with what we've been taught. Our educa-tional system provides us with a false sense of confidence that the more we know, the more successful we'll be. I believe, however, that what we don't know—once we know we don't know it—represents a huge, untapped opportunity.

So much in Italy in the years before I arrived was old and tired—classical, yes, but also boring. The old ways needed shaking up. So in the early 1980s, a group of Italian designers and architects—called Memphis and led by Ettore Sottsass and Allesandro Mendini—came up with a radical new sensibility, almost like throwing a cultural bomb. In the end this movement was all about revitalizing design as a tool in commerce, a lesson I've never forgotten. Members of Memphis got product designers in Italy to wake up and use their homegrown talents in fresh new ways. They saw the importance of having a vision and a carefully developed aesthetic, but they also understood the need to partner with factory owners and other industrial leaders. The only way for artists and architects to get the fruits of their innovation out to the world was to use Italian industry.

It was all great fun. The sensibility was wide open and all-encompassing. There was room for everything: found objects, references to things current and historical, edited by no one. We were all aware of the work done by Marcel Duchamp on the idea of "found" art, especially his "readymade" series starting in 1915, featuring everything from a shovel and a broom to a hat rack and a bicycle wheel and, most controversial, a urinal, which he signed "R. Mutt." We knew about Man Ray's work in the same area and the "found art" exhibitions arranged by Arturo Schwartz in New York.

Those early experiences in Italy made me feel like a kid who discovered a cache of new toys—whatever toys he wanted. Growing up humble in Brooklyn, I thought of myself almost as a New York street rat, which of course meant I got a great education in life. To this day I think of that street-rat persona as a big part of who I am. Life with my Italian family gave me a taste of what it's like to live well with style and design, history and meaning, art and beauty. Ultimately, my creative personality became a fusion of those two sides of me. You see it in my language, which can be coarse and direct but also thoughtful and inspiring. To this day I take the notion of being a gentleman very seriously, and for that I thank my family in Italy. They opened doors for me and opened my eyes to another way of life. I watched and absorbed their style and their ways and let it affect me positively. They opened my mind. They took my natural hyperkinetic creative and intellectual energy and helped give it a direction. That helped me find a way to *live* my passion, not just think about it. Once my Italian family was part of my life, I never worried about whether I might take my passion too far. In fact, this is why my inspiration for hosiery advertising was Michelangelo. Yes, that Michelangelo.

CHAPTER 11

The Genius of Michelangelo

WE ALL TEND TO TAKE great artists for granted, figures who, like Michelangelo, were centuries ahead of their time and laid the foundation for so much to come. I think we would all benefit from paying more attention to the masters, to look at their work with a fresh eye and learn from it. From Michelangelo, for example, we can learn that when we look at a sculpture, or at any piece of art, we're really looking at a series of shadows and contrasts. The content lives in the shapes and the spaces between the form. We are vividly aware of what's *not* there. This is especially clear in the example of the *Pietà,* Michelangelo's masterpiece of sculpture, his unspeakably beautiful evocation of the prone form of Jesus after he was crucified, lying on the lap of his mother, Mary.

If you look carefully at the statue, reading the folds and the chiffon on the sash and on the actual drapery, or if you're looking at the fingers just under the arm, you will notice eight different points of blackness. One is the left side of Mary's head, one is underneath Jesus' knee, one is on the back of his left leg, two are in the drape areas, and one is under the finger area, one is on the backdrop, and one is on the bottom. The points of blackness are visual cues that shape how we perceive what we are seeing. The black in the background allows us to see the shape in the foreground. The negative space serves as a road map for the eye. If there was only white on white, we wouldn't be able to *read* the images. It takes daring and command to master the use of shadow, and most sculptors don't even try. But using this technique, Michelangelo is able to give us an array of points that make the eye frame what it is seeing in exactly the way he intended. The effect is so masterfully conceived that if we did an overlay of the golden section, you would see that he was working with a perfect sense of proportion and perspective to create this contrast.

So many of the techniques that Michelangelo was using, and so much of the immense knowledge from which he was drawing, were never really transferred to modern-day art. He imbues the sculpture with a dynamic quality that gives people the feeling they are looking at a living, breathing Mary, which fits with Michelangelo's decision to portray her as young and beautiful. As he told his fellow sculptor Ascanio Condivi, who wrote an authorized biography of Michelangelo: "Do you not know that chaste women stay fresh much more than those who are not chaste? How much more in the case of the Virgin, who had never experienced the least lascivious desire that might change her body?"

The dynamic effect is so strong that if you get close and look at Mary, you would swear that her bottom lip is quivering. It's not static at all. Mary's left hand is raised, open palmed, rather than touching the leg of Jesus, a symbolic representation of her acceptance of God's will. Put it together and you have her hand held open in a kind of prayer, the head quivering, the almost disheveled look of her clothing, which conveys a sense of the chaos of the time.

Then there is the powerful, over-the-top artistic decision that Michelangelo made with the *Pietà*, unlike any decision he had ever made before. At the base he leaves the actual chiseled stone to show viewers that this is a work of and by man. In back you see untouched, unpolished stone. Michelangelo was stating that this was a human endeavor, demanding that you know and share the struggle of creation. As Michelangelo said, "Every block of stone has a statue inside it and it is the task of the sculptor to discover it."

What is most amazing to me about the sculpture, though, what really starts to work on you as you spend time there in the dark, quiet air of Saint Peter's Basilica, taking in the details, is how many liberties Michelangelo took for artistic effect. Keep in mind, he was only twenty-two years old when he started working on it in 1498. He had already spent months dissecting cadavers in the local morgue to gain a deeper understanding of human anatomy, defying the dictates of the church in doing so. He'd built his knowledge of anatomical perspective from the hundreds of cadavers he'd taken apart. We've seen the pencil drawings he made of those cut body parts to educate himself.

So when he deliberately plays with true scale or true proportion, he knows precisely what impression he is creating, and the effect is that much stronger. He uses his skill and his vision to look to something beyond the literal truth, aspiring to more than a literal depiction. Drawing from Michelangelo and other great Renaissance artists, I have always tried in my own work to depict the kind of beauty and perfection that the consumer—or the viewer—aspires to find, whether or not it is a literal depiction of reality. For inspiration, I always go back to the *Pietà*.

If you look at the folds of fabric around Mary's legs, especially her left leg, you can make out a pattern—a depiction of a palm with a stem. Incredible! The fabric would never drape on the body that way! The effect is of a forceful central column there, which holds society aloft. Call it the mother, the beauty of humanity; call it innocence, an innocence you can understand and approach. It represents the stability of society at that time—the stability of the church.

If you stare at the details of the outstretched arm of Jesus and look at the way the light reflects off the surface, you realize that no artist has ever depicted a muscle, a tendon, a vein, like this. You start to realize the fragility of the endeavor. If you look under the knee at the hamstring muscle, it is soft, not taut the way the muscle under a knee would naturally be. It would tighten up right there. Michelangelo rendered it concave. It's got a two-inch turn-in. You see the contrast lines. You see how it makes the knee look sad. You see the beauty and the sensuality of the foot and how it hangs limply, almost droops. It's so extraordinary it's painful. It can bring you down to your knees and make you cry. But that pain, that beauty, are the sorts of feeling you need to keep alive inside yourself so you can draw on them later—as I discovered when I had the chance to work with an up-and-coming designer named Donna Karan.

CHAPTER 12

How the Past Can Inspire
Your Future

WHEN YOU HAVE THE MOST on the line and the least
going for you, you learn the most about yourself. That is particularly true when it comes to personal change, when every
step can seem so daunting, so potentially difficult. The best
way to approach such challenges is to approach them in the
way you start out in a first job, when you can't rely on your
reputation or on your track record to speak for you.

When I was young and hungry, I started a small agency
with my friend from Michael Graves's office, Ted Bickford,
called Arnell-Bickford, in the early 1980s thanks to a loan I
was able to line up from the Citibank branch at the corner of
Park Avenue and Fifty-seventh Street. I chose that bank because it was so inspiring to see that address on my business
checks. I was so new, so unknown, I knew that the only way
to establish credibility with my vendors was to have a presti-

gious address on every check so people who had never heard of me would be less likely to question whether there was money in the agency's account to pay the bills.

I have the Swiss architect and marketing entrepreneur Paul Gredinger to thank for giving me a boost at a critical time in my profession. Gredinger had founded a very successful advertising agency in Zurich, Switzerland, called GGK. One day he showed up at my office on 100 Grand Street, soon after I had opened the doors for business. He wore a thick brown tweed three-piece suit. The fabric looked like the thick woolen fabric that mountain villagers used to make their clothes. I found out later that he wore this type of suit every day.

Paul was a big, burly man, easy-going and friendly; he squinted when he smiled, which he did a lot.

"I read an article about you guys," he told me. "What do you need to get started? How much money?"

This is miraculous, I thought to myself. But taking one look at Paul Gredinger, I sensed that everything about his appearance said he was for real.

"We could use a hundred thousand dollars," I said candidly.

He nodded. And the next day he wrote a check for that amount, a loan. He never asked for a contract or a formal piece of paper confirming that I'd received the money. In fact, he never came by the agency again. Toward the end of that first year, I was able to pay him back in full. Later I read an admiring account of working with Paul in a book called *Reaching for Advertising Excellence*, by Morton Kirschner. Kirschner wrote of Paul, "He was always grateful for any little service that you gave him and only seemed to be interested in the creative work. He believed strongly in change and he felt that any change actually created opportunities and opportunity was advantageous for the future."

I guess Paul and I were fated to meet. You can never predict why things happen to you. That hundred thousand dollars that Paul Gredinger gave us, no strings attached, no questions asked, was the money that kept us alive during the initial growth of the business. It mattered. But even more important was the way Gredinger went about offering the money. He did not question me or put me on the spot in any way.

I began to put what I had learned in Italy to practical use when I had the opportunity to work with the designer Donna Karan. After Anne Klein died in 1974, Donna took over at the helm. In 1983 she had a huge success with the launch of Anne Klein II, a second line that was intended as an affordable option for working women, adapting the main line but using different fabric. It was just a matter of time before Donna went out to start her own label. When she did, she needed to find a way to launch her new line with a bang. That meant she needed a great logo—not just any logo, but a logo that announced a fresh and sexy and stylish and sophisticated new brand.

Donna wanted to launch her new company with new talent, and that included me. She liked to discover people, and that opened the door for me and my team. Dawn Mello, who was close to Donna, was already a fan of my work, based on an in-store poster project I did for Bergdorf Goodman. Donna and Dawn especially liked a series I did with the *Vogue* photographer Denis Piel, who liked to say that his whole approach to photography was based on voyeurism. He was probably best known for one amazingly sexy shot he took of Andie MacDowell sitting back with her frilly white dress inching up her thighs.

I had two meetings with Donna, including one at her little temporary studio on the south side of Bryant Park near the New York Public Library, talking over the counter in her kitchen, drinking a lot of coffee, and exchanging a lot of excited ideas. The energy between us was phenomenal—I floated out of those meetings. This was a huge opportunity for Donna, and for my agency. Moreover, I had a feeling that I knew exactly what would be right for Donna. I went home that night in an exhilarating haze of creativity and started wildly cutting and pasting images of great old black-and-white photographs that I knew were what we wanted to use for the inspiration for the marketing campaign.

I cut and pasted shots of the great Edward Steichen and his haunting, blurry early photographs of New York City in the years after World War I, in which he had served as the head of an aerial photography unit. I cut and pasted Alfred Stieglitz photographs, Berenice Abbott photos, and many images from the early editions of Stieglitz's *Camera Work*. I cut and pasted everything from that era I could find and put it together with the Optima typeface lettering I was sure we should use for the logo. I wanted to capture *that* New York, the New York of those haunting, edgy photographs, iconic images that showed the city's true spirit—Central Park, Fifth Avenue, the Brooklyn Bridge. I wanted to capture the New York of Truman

Capote and *Breakfast at Tiffany's*, the New York of Audrey Hepburn as Holly Golightly in the classic Blake Edwards movie of Capote's book, and the New York of the immigrants with their first view of the New York skyline seen from their boat arriving at Ellis Island. A New York of hope, power, art, dreams, and chaos.

A lot of people and influences play a role in any genuine success. Denis Piel understood what I was after when I described the blurry images of New York in the spirit of Steichen, pulsing and throbbing, to give consumers the experience of a customer on a shopping spree in New York, that indescribable New York energy.

Donna was a lifelong New Yorker and so clearly a product of her environment. That was who she was. She was an embodiment of the sophistication of New York that women across the country felt, that sense they had of a visit to Manhattan, offering a glimpse of a world of glamorous couture clothes on a shopping tour of the city. I knew customers from coast to coast would relate to that iconography, that environment. After all, it was the inspiration for Donna's look and her clothes. All I had to do was to capture it in a modern way that would impact Donna's customers. As Donna always said, "I *am* my customers," which was undeniably true. It's what gave her a leg up on her competitors, nearly all of whom were men.

I went downtown early in the morning to pick up Denis in SoHo, on Broadway, way before sunrise. I had asked him to bring along handheld cameras like Leicas, the same camera Steichen used. Then we headed uptown in a cab. Wanting to lower my sky-high expectations for the shoot, Denis kept saying, "I don't know if I can get it." I did my best to put him at ease. "Let's just go. If you don't get it, you don't get it. Let's just give it our best shot." But I knew he would get it. He was able to capture reality in a powerful and vivid way.

We piled out of the cab at the corner of Fifth Avenue and Fifty-seventh Street, exactly where Holly Golightly gets out of the cab in a famous scene in the movie, and I asked Denis to dive right in and start clicking away. We started with the energy of the speed of cars, the feeling and the mood of blurriness, of chaos, of the over-the-top, overwhelming spirit of New York City. Instead of a quiet moment like Hepburn enjoyed in the movie, we decided to do the opposite. We decided to do Holly Goheavy.

It was very high-energy. The impact of those reportage-style photographs in the spirit of Steichen, Stieglitz, Abbott, Weegee, and Margaret Bourke-White; the famous skyline frozen in time, historically correct portrayals of the modern pioneering spirit of this great Dutch colony, reminded the world of the greatness of New York. The photographs were at once heroic and historic. But most important, they were a reflection of the fantasy of the energized environment that all of Donna's customers wanted to occupy and live in. The images held up a kind of mirror to consumers, a reflection of their self-worth and desires, the rich possibilities of their lives. The photos screamed: "Join me!" "Take me!" "Use me!" "Visit me!" "Have me!" "I'm yours!" They invited the modern woman to take her rightful place in culture and society, which was always Donna's dream. And, most avant garde of all, there was no clothing to be found in those ads. It was the first time that I can remember that a fashion spread had no model and no product. To some people in the industry, shooting an ad that way meant you couldn't afford models. I didn't care about those assumptions.

I had learned form and content, black and white, from the great Michelangelo: I trusted the wisdom of his example as I carved out a place for the Donna Karan New York brand in the national psyche. For the picture we used of Brooklyn Bridge for the campaign, I tried to depict Brooklyn Bridge through the eyes of a sleepy boy of fourteen who has just climbed out of his grandpa's car early in the morning and looks up to see the dark, murky late-night outline of that great bridge. It was an image burned into my soul as a boy. I wanted to give Donna something that would be true and real from me for the campaign. It was the only thing I knew.

Donna and her most trusted right hand, Patti Cohen, were ecstatic when they saw the images.

"This is it!" They were crying and screaming, "Peeetah!" as only New Yorkers can draw out.

Donna had wanted to create fashion that was both beautiful and functional, the essence of her customers' needs. I was able to fashion a campaign based on the power of her message; it helped to build one of the largest fashion empires in the world.

Our work led to a series of ads depicting Donna's alter ego, model Rosemary McGrotha, running for presidential office on the campaign trail, showing that women could run society as well as any man. Years later *Harper's Bazaar* magazine ran an article and photo spread titled "Why a Woman Should Be President," four years before Hillary Clinton narrowly missed landing the Democratic presidential nomination. "Taking a cue from Donna Karan's legendary Peter Lindbergh–lensed 1992 ad campaign, which depicted a woman as president," the magazine explained in 2004 about my campaign for Donna, "*Bazaar* cast Ellen DeGeneres as the U.S. commander in chief. Here, she tells us, in her witty way, what a female leader would bring to our country—style, grace and a whole lot of pantsuits." It was a wonderful confirmation of the work I had done for Donna and the existing importance today of showcasing women in the powerful way they deserve to be seen.

Everything Donna touched seemed to turn to gold. So in 1987, Hanes decided to launch a Donna Karan line of hosiery, introducing a heavier, more opaque type of panty hose. "Everyone here thought we were on drugs," my friend Cathy Volker, already a Donna Karan devotee and president of Hanes Hosiery, later recalled to *Time* magazine. Cathy wanted to give women a little Donna Karan for the bottom half of their bodies, for the very affordable sum of fourteen bucks. You didn't have to shell out thousands of dollars for couture Donna, yet you could say you were wearing Donna Karan. It was brilliant. And it exploded Donna's business. It expanded her line from the couture floor to the main floor, next to perfume and cosmetics.

Once again, the line's success depended on an ad campaign to develop a new way of looking at women's hosiery. I had an idea of what I wanted to do—crazy and bold as I was sure it would sound to people—but only an idea. So I went to see my friend David Finn, a photographer and public-relations executive who had spent years documenting Renaissance statues.

My thoughts went back to Vatican City, back to Saint Peter's Basilica, to that trance I fell into during all those hours I spent staring at Michelangelo's *Pietà*. As I looked at David's collection of pictures in preparation for the shoot for the first Donna Karan Hosiery campaign, my mind kept flashing back to the *Pietà*.

I decided that for this hosiery ad, there would be no hosiery. We would photograph a photograph of a bare leg, using classic lighting. I wanted the model undressed. The sensibility I wanted to evoke was one in which the hosiery was almost presold, before you even got into the store. I had waited years for the chance to take some of that breathtaking beauty I felt standing in front of the *Pietà* and give some of it back to the world. The photographer Denis Piel and I were on the same wavelength.

The photograph was perfect. Once we explained the concept to Donna and showed her Denis's shot, she claimed it was the most extraordinary picture she had ever seen. Later, at the 1987 Council of Fashion Designers of America Fashion Awards, Arnell-Bickford received a special award for the ad. Someone at the ceremony said, "What a great way to make the customer run and go buy a product"—because the customer worries that it won't be there if she takes too long. By not showing the hosiery itself, we were able to spark demand among women who wanted to experience the Donna Karan name and brand.

Having spent so many years mulling over what Michelangelo had done and why, I had a very clear sense of what the ad needed to look like. He had achieved perfection. So it made sense to go back to that perfection, back to the notion of a bare leg. There are a lot of things in life that can get me excited, and when I find one of those things, I hold on to it and build from it.

I'm not saying that you have to be moved by the *Pietà* as I am, or share my passion for Renaissance art. My point is this: Whatever you take in becomes part of you. Give yourself permission to tap into that storage vault in your life and career. Your own capital grows from your constant aggregation of knowledge and experiences.

If you're not tapping into what you've experienced, as I did with the blurry black-and-white pictures of New York for the Donna Karan campaign, you're missing an extraordinary opportunity to enrich your career, your work, and your life. My passion for architecture and art and art history, my quest to understand the meaning and purpose behind that history, helped to fuel a vision that allowed Donna Karan to sell hosiery for Hanes at an affordable price. It gave women all over the country, from all walks of life, the invitation they had been craving to join the party and head out into the world wearing Donna, to become part of a movement. That is the power of the past. I began my career in architecture and used that knowledge to become an architect of my life. It is important to work with your strengths.

CHAPTER 13

Fueling the Imagination

MY WORK WITH DONNA tapped into my abiding love of New York. While developing Donna's brand, at times it felt as if I were breathing fresh life into New York itself—looking deeper into what New York was and what it meant to people, how it grew into a city like no other. I celebrated its status as the greatest man-made spectacle in the world, drawing tourists from every spot on the globe. But at the same time, it is a city built for everyone, with a grid of democratically numbered streets and avenues, which makes it easy for visitors and immigrants to navigate, whatever their language. The idea of New York has been all about reinventing one's life, making money and creating a career, building one's fortune amid an ever-expanding skyline. It is a city built on optimism.

New York has always been about being the greatest, and the worst, about both anguish and joy. As Frank Sinatra sang in the movie *New York, New York,* if you can make it here, you'll make it anywhere. For centuries, the city has been a magnet for finance, the media, immigrants, and raw energy. In 1790 it was already the largest city in the United States, ahead of Philadelphia and Boston. Its population doubled to more than 60,000 in 1800, and 1.2 million by 1880. New York prospered by always being ready to embrace the new even as it retained the best of its past, in an endless cycle of birth and rebirth.

The Donna Karan brand soared on its organic link to that New York of promise and aspiration, of real lives and real women. And we knew that we could take that further.

It became clear that given the success of the DK New York couture line, Donna needed to launch a second, less high-end, line. That was the way for her to grow as a business and as a creative spirit. Donna challenged me to come up with a bold new idea for the second line. But she handed me no creative brief. Donna just did what Donna does, talking about her vision. It was up to me to hold the mirror in front of her vision again.

For many years, clothes designers had named second lines by simply putting a "2" after their name and settling for an affordable imitation of the designs in the original line, but done with less precious fabric. For most designers, the secondary lines are an afterthought. But not Donna. She wanted to make a big splash by giving women, her customers, what they needed and wanted from their clothes.

We chose to use the second line to expose another side of Donna, rather than designing cheaper versions of her couture line. As Donna said, "I like caviar, but I also like pizza. *Why* can't fashion give women both—and all in one brand?" I knew she was right, so I had some fun with the idea.

I showed Donna a chart I'd created for her with a photo of caviar against a pizza. The caption read, "Women like caviar *and* pizza, too." We were working with the casual side of her personality, going from a weekday look to more of a weekend look. At the time, the weekend sensibility was creeping more and more into the fashion and lifestyle choices people were making from coast to coast. There had been an enormous push by Mickey Drexler and his team at The Gap to make casual Friday a fashion trend. It grew out of the rise of California style, especially as the informality of the New Economy and Silicon Valley began to pick up steam.

Donna was looking for a simple focus. She knew what the product was going to be, because she had created it out of her own closet, the jeans and the big wrapped shawl and that classy-but-casual Donna look everyone came to know and love. We wanted to get that all across in a simple message. But how? A lot of lines carried the designer's initials, but they were mostly fashion main lines, like YSL. Initials are a form of personal signature and evoke a designer's intimate relationship with his or her customers. An abbreviation seems more casual, almost like a nickname, like NYPD. I went out and began to photograph all the abbreviation logos of New York for inspiration.

Late one night I was working in the studio with a bunch of my colleagues when we decided to try something that hadn't been done before to capture that casual spirit of abbreviation: I spelled out DKNY in bold Helvetica letters; and we placed a small dot under the "D" and the "K" and the "N" and the "Y," so that people would see the correspondence with "Donna Karan New York." We wanted to be 100 percent sure that the customer would understand instantly that this line was a part of the Donna Karan family. The most critical thing, we realized, was to make sure that there was no separation for the customer from the author of the brand, Donna Karan. It had to be crystal clear that DKNY was part of her original thinking, that it was the same designer, the same woman, only another side of her.

I took the old photographs from Stieglitz and Steichen and the others and put them together to form a big ad hoc newspaper, three feet tall by two and a half feet wide. And in there I had the whole DKNY identity and logo development—how we would develop products around that identity in everything from clothing and jewelry to stationery, from the design and style of Donna's retail stores to the advertising. It was all conceived together, organically, in one fell swoop. I put a big DKNY on the cover, eye-catching and bold and different. And I knew I had it—I was ready to present what I felt was an exciting and iconic image of Donna the brand to the woman herself.

The big moment came late in the day one Thursday or Friday. It was already dark outside. I remember pausing at the entrance to her offices, wondering how Donna and Patti would react. As soon as Donna saw my work, she started crying. Then Patti began to cry, and I was about to cry but fought it back. Then she reached out and hugged me, calling me a genius—although, truth be told, if anyone was a genius among us, it was Donna. The tears began to flow.

That was her way of sharing authorship of this remarkable moment. In all successful marketing, if you do your job right, nothing that you're presenting should feel like yours. It's *theirs*. They wear it. They claim it. They own it. This basic act of transferring authorship forms the foundation of all great branding campaigns.

In the ideal case, customers adopt the idea or conception, so that it *feels* like *theirs*. If you go to the auto showroom to test-drive a Range Rover or BMW, you never feel that you are driving someone else's car, even though of course the car doesn't belong to you. You feel as though you're driving *your car*. Truly great marketing leads customers to adopt the product at first sight and make it their own and invite it into their lives. They go beyond a transaction—buying—and give the product a role in their lives. In short: They *join* the product.

This leap of faith has to occur spontaneously. You can only prepare the right circumstances, the right environment. You can only get potential customers interested. You might be able to get them to *want* the product. But you can't make them *invite* it into their lives. They have to do that themselves. You may never know the details of why or when or how that occurs. You have only a general sense, based on instinct, demographics, projections. But we seemed to have achieved that with Donna and our work on DKNY.

I approached the same model who had appeared as Donna's alter ego, Rosemary McGrotha, in Donna's earlier ads. We photographed her running barefoot in jeans on a beach in the Hamptons, and strolling along at the old Twenty-sixth Street flea market on a Sunday afternoon under a warm cape wrapped over jeans. Hiring the same model was part of the answer to connecting Donna's new line to Donna's life, mirroring her activities and clothes choices over the course of the week. Lifestyle campaigns, however, had been done before. Simply giving the public another version of Donna was not going to be enough.

To make a bold statement, I created a seven-story painted wall in New York's historic Soho district, the heart of the original light-manufacturing district at the turn of the nineteenth century. There at the corner of Houston Street and Broadway we made a big, powerfully visible statement with the four letters: DKNY. We cut and pasted a montage of an aerial photograph of New York City looking south, and an image of the Statue of Liberty draped in all her majesty but with a certain casualness to her wrapped, pleated gown, not unlike the way Donna showed women on her runway with a draped, cashmere overthrow.

This wall created a new icon for the city and for Donna. And so Donna's new DKNY global brand was launched, breaking the mold of her Donna Karan collection price points. DKNY went on to earn a billion dollars. Thank you, Dutch settlers, I thought to myself. Thank you, Robert Moses and John D. Rockefeller. Thank you, Walter Chrysler, with your majestic 1930s art deco Chrysler Building. Thank you, Woody Allen, and thank you, New York and New Yorkers.

* * *

The point of all this? You have to find out what works for *you*. You have to look for images or associations or values that you can harvest or cull from your past that can act as giant levers to move your present career and situation. Finding that lever is not always easy. Doing so can take a lot of time and a lot of effort. But when you find it, I think you'll consider the search worthwhile.

When Donna first hired me to create her brand identity, we did a ton of research, as all good designers do. We studied other high-end fashion labels, brands, and identities as they appeared on clothes, on tags, in stores, and in various ads and other communications. The important fashion brands anchored themselves in a city, a specific place, a specific location, a specific feeling: for Christian Dior, Paris; for Giorgio Armani, Milan; for Asprey, London. What we did not see was a fashion designer with a brand anchored in the fashion capital of the world: New York.

It seemed fitting that Donna, a woman from Queens, take pride in her home. People began to "see" New York through her designs and imagery, through her take on the city. They let every woman get involved in the brand and make it her own. Adding "New York" to the brand name was not about defining "New York style"; it was about Donna's personal expression and vision of New York.

We fueled the imagination by focusing on what is not there in the Hanes hosiery ad that we did for Donna, which simply showed a beautiful leg in a seductive pose. It allowed women to imagine the feeling of the hosiery for themselves.

Above: My grandparents Nathan and Ada Hutt in Rockaway, New York, circa 1920. They were always fit and stylish.

Right: Me at age six, still unaware of the impact food would have on my life.

Top: With mentor Jack Warnecke: *(left)* at 350 pounds at his Russian River, California, ranch and *(right)* at 180 pounds in my New York studio.

Bottom: I got so big that when shooting advertising campaigns for my clients, I used my stomach as a tripod.

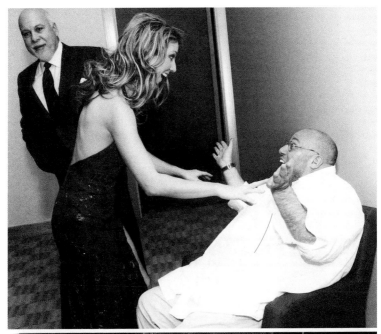

Top: With Céline Dion and her husband, René, at the apex of my weight . . .
Bottom: . . . and after my weight loss, back with Céline and René in Las Vegas at
Caesars Palace.

Top: With architect Frank Gehry at New York's Lowell Hotel in 1997.

Bottom: With Frank Gehry in his Los Angeles studio after my "rebranding."

Opposite, bottom: Sylvester Stallone is always an inspiration to me and one of my "fan club" members who encouraged and supported my journey. Watching him in *Rocky* time and time again helped me to keep up the fight.

Above: At his Alliance for a Healthier Generation event in Harlem, New York, President Bill Clinton asked me to stand up as he told my weight-loss story to a reporter who had challenged him by asking if people could really change their habits enough to lose substantial weight. I was his proof.

Patti Cohen of the Donna Karan Company taught me early on in my career that everyone needs a fan club to recognize and affirm their success. She did this for me by awarding me the job of branding Donna Karan and developing a second line known today as DKNY.

Martha Stewart told me not to buy new clothes, but instead to tailor my existing ones until I was ready to reveal my weight loss as part of my new brand of self. The "shock and awe" effect of seeing a completely new me in terms of weight and style left people speechless.

Universally loved by all, Peter Lopez is the ultimate fan and supporter. I consider him my personal CBO (chief branding officer). He is always aware of the importance of keeping my personal brand "on strategy."

Alfredo Pecora of Brioni told me I needed new pants when the two back pockets on my khakis began to merge into one due to being taken in so many times.

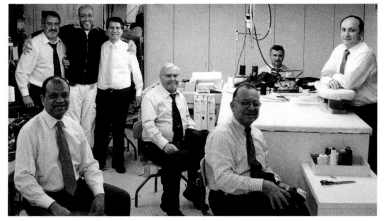

With the expert tailors at Brioni, who were both supporters and fans. Every time they took in another few inches, it felt like a party in the sewing room.

With Bob Nardelli and architect Frank Gehry. It is important to remember that like attracts like. If you want the chance to be inspired by big thinkers, think big yourself.

Next to the Peapod electric car with Bob Nardelli. Everyone needs someone like Bob in their life—someone who believes in you, almost more than you do in yourself.

Muhammad Ali declared he was the Greatest, and therefore he became the Greatest. His inspiration helped me declare myself a thin man, then work to achieve that goal.

Above left: Eunice Kennedy Shriver, founder of the Special Olympics, told me that her brother JFK would have loved me because my feet never touch the ground. Encouragement like this is what makes you fly higher. *Above right:* Edwin and Giannita, the manager and head seamstress of Prada in New York, stuck by me as we tailored and changed my wardrobe over the course of a few years as my waist size went from 68 to 28 inches.

Above left: I have favorite tailors everywhere! Here I am in Rome at Albertelli, where Valentino and a host of other impeccably dressed men get their clothing fitted and perfected. *Above right:* With André Leon Talley, my friend and style guru, waiting to pick up tailored clothes after my final weight loss. I'm now 150 pounds.

This kind of advertising can make a bigger, more powerful point than focusing on the object itself, which can sometimes circumscribe your dreams and stop you from reaching out for them. There's so much to see that hasn't been depicted yet! So much to imagine that hasn't been imagined! Don't be afraid to live in the world of original ideas. Don't be afraid to unleash your own imagination. When you do, remember, no one can tell you that you're wrong.

CHAPTER 14

Don't Ask: *Compel*

WHEN YOU DECIDE it's time to look at specific things that you want to change in your life or career, you need to know *how* to bring about change. But first, you need to know what change you want to bring about in yourself, and *why*. The starting point for any effective branding or rebranding—of yourself or of anyone or anything—is authenticity. You must feel comfortable in your own skin. You want to arrive at a place where you are not asking anything of anyone, instead are *compelling* others to go along with you on your journey of self-discovery, *compelling* them to accept the new you and to do so whole-heartedly.

This means one thing for companies, which need believability to compel people to buy their brands. But what does it mean for you, in your life? For starters, it means you should stop asking questions such as "Is this okay?" or "Do you like my clothes?" or "Did you notice my haircut?" Stop looking for feedback that will only give you an excuse to adjust who you are to others' expectations. It's true that fitting into the norm is the easy way to go, but don't do it at the expense of being who you are. Your goals are to be who you want to be and compel others to accept you and see you in that way.

The verb *compel* is an apt choice. Don't ask, "How do you want me to be?" *Asking* reveals a lack of confidence and denies personal expression. *Compelling* says, "See me the way I want you to see me."

Russell Simmons calls this mind-set "Do You!" Would anyone have believed, in the early 1980s when a young Russell was managing the influential hip-hop group Run DMC and fighting his way to success, that he would become a role model for a vegan, yoga, and meditation-driven lifestyle? Inconceivable. But today when you see him, hear him, *listen* to him, you know you are in the presence of a guru. He compels you to see him in this way. And it's not because he's wearing yoga pants and a stretchy top, along with his baseball cap, Phat Farm clothes, and sneakers. His attitude compels you. His self-confidence compels you.

In my work for McDonald's I realized how important it is to pull people into a brand, to compel them to join in. It is the one sure way to revitalize a brand image for a youthful audience—to drive preference through association. It's about aspiration. It's about being part of pop culture.

McDonald's needed to bolster its image and shift the brand from a value burger chain to a value-centric food chain with cool, hip associations. The brand needed a style makeover. It needed to be seen as a cool place to grab a good meal, not just a good place to grab a cheap meal. McDonald's always had multiple advertising agencies and consultants working for the corporation. One of the international agencies came up with the brand line "I'm Lovin' It." Charlie Bell and Larry Light, who were running McDonald's marketing and communications at that time, saw "lovin' it" as a great way to give the brand a consumer voice and a more friendly and emotional appeal.

I was brought in to help them define the new spirit of McDonald's based on the "I'm Lovin' It" attitude. We created a fully integrated program that included everything from designing new packaging, new sandwich wraps, and new employee uniforms to new store signage, new store design, new mascot characters, and even an updated Ronald McDonald. Everything was getting a face-lift. But to launch all this with the real pop-culture tremor it deserved, we needed a way to break through to young adults and get them to notice McDonald's again. They needed to stop taking it for granted and think about it in a fresh way.

Enter Justin Timberlake. Justin was our answer to bringing sexy back to a brand that needed to reinvigorate itself. We signed Justin as the voice of the brand, and he wrote a song featuring the "I'm Lovin' It" slogan and a memorable tune that could be used to link the slogan to the brand. Commercials with the music played on TV and the radio. The association with Justin Timberlake helped McDonald's bring new value to its customers and make style an integral part of its brand personality. McDonald's association with Justin pulled in a younger, hipper audience, and compelled them to see Mc-Donald's in a new way. It's one thing to have a great line and a whole other for a pop icon to promote it and perform it.

When Donna Karan launched her DK collection business, she compelled consumers to see the New York working woman through her eyes. No more man-tailored suits and white shirts with big bows to replace the necktie. No more women trying to channel a more feminine version of a man's suit. Donna's vision compelled us to see women at work in body suits, form-flattering skirts with shawls, wraps, and gold jewelry that could take you from day to night. Donna's woman was still smart, but now she was her own woman with her own "uniform." Donna didn't rely on research to find out what working women wanted to wear to the office or how they dealt with going to a cocktail party or a dinner after work. She had her own, unique personal vision, and she compelled other women to join her in this vision.

In designing the new Pepsi logo, I needed to compel consumers to see a familiar brand in a more personally appealing way. I wanted to invite the consumer into the Pepsi world. I saw the Pepsi logo as a corporate symbol, not as a pure expression of the brand for the consumer. So my team gently transitioned it from a globe with a white wave through the center to a face with a smile. Same shape, same colors. Same structure as the original logo. But now it had the added dimension of genuine expression. What could be more compelling than a smile? Your mind is the most powerful tool imaginable in bringing about change. Change your mind, and change your life.

* * *

If you can compel others to see you as you want to be seen, instead of asking them to see you differently, I believe the sky is *not* the limit. But how can you compel others to see you as you want to be seen? How can you reflect your best self to the world at large? There are three key marketing principles that any person or brand must apply in order to achieve positive change.

Creating Invitational Mind-sets

People who remain stuck in the mind-set that their relationships with others are transactional—based on what they can do for others or others can do for them—are going to have a hard time here. Function and convenience are not a replacement for caring. Just because you can get something fast and easy does not mean that it doesn't also need meaning. Your headline should no longer be "Is This Who You Want Me to Be?" Instead, think along the lines of "We Are Creating a Party and You Are Invited!" Make it fun; make it a little crazy. The point is, you have to *earn* allegiance, attention, recognition, and admiration. How? By doing something from the heart and for the heart.

People who do what I do for a living have to find a way to *compel* people to want to support them. That means working to establish an invitational mind-set from start to finish. Too many people in the corporate world talk about transactions; not enough talk about invitations or destinations. I'm a firm believer that most people want to get invited to the party.

And they're anxious about getting on the list. You just have to create an invitation and get it to the right people. Hopefully the party will build from there.

Concurrent Model Versus Sequential Model

This distinction applies more to corporations than to individuals. Big corporations generally have a lot of departments, and departments have handoff gates: This department does one thing and then passes off to the next department, and so on. Marketing drives one thing, then hands it off to research, then back to marketing, then on to design, and so on. My take on that? Throw it all out the window and get everyone working—and thinking—together! Get everyone to think and see and, yes, feel as one about how to solve problems and build on the vision of a product or company. By slowing the process down, you are speeding it up, building a high-performing accountable *team*. The most interesting part of that Shift in approach is that now everyone on your team can learn and grow and develop his or her abilities and strengths.

To work concurrently, first get everyone at the table together to form a strong sense of shared mission. Sparks tend to fly as people get used to the new way of doing things. Top professionals who have been doing their jobs in a certain way for years, even decades, are being asked to revise their ways of thinking and communicating. People often feel threatened, as if their expertise is being stripped away. A person in sales usually has very little background in or knowledge of how to design a brand identity, and a manufacturing person usually knows little about sales. Both have been operating on a need-to-know basis and have only limited understanding of what other departments do. Giving them a voice on the complete development of a product or line is like throwing open a window and letting in a strong breeze. Now everyone can breathe. Unfortunately, some people are put off by the draft.

The *New York Times* published an article in September 1999 mentioning the concept of "holistic marketing" or "fully integrated marketing." Robert Wehling, Procter & Gamble's global marketing officer, explained it as "looking at all the forms of communicating, bonding with our customers, whatever it takes: direct mail, public relations, Internet advertising, new media, traditional advertising."

My company has been practicing something similar for more than thirty years. Whether by default or by coincidence, from our first days in working with Donna Karan, taking the cues I learned from architecture, we were able to help to shape boutique design and in-store experience, packaging, identity, advertising, logo design, communications, and product and retail design for Donna's very first product introduction, including dresses, belts, bags, T-shirts, and scarves. We didn't know that what we were doing would later be called "fully integrated" marketing. We were just doing what worked, making sure all aspects of the brand were talking to one another in a harmonious and supportive fashion. It was simply common sense. And other great designers were doing it, too—Ralph Lauren and Calvin Klein, and in Europe, Chanel, Fendi, and Gucci—all intuitively integrating their grand stories to create a look and experience that was seamless. This is what great branders do.

Part of that obviously had to do with Donna's belief that she has a single voice in marketing for her line, not a complicated idea for someone who produced dresses and bags and belts and coats under her name. And she assumed her partner on the branding side would implement that idea. This kind of integrated marketing came naturally to me, given my background in architecture, where from the beginning I learned to draw from and understand different disciplines. To me, great architecture is the embodiment of getting engineering and interiors and structural and mechanical considerations all working together to form a seamless, harmonious, unique experience for people. As a result, I was one of the first to talk about "brand architecture." It was just an efficient way to over-communicate all the touch points of a corporation's message and ensure uniformity in the language used to convey the essence of a company's message.

Using Marketing to Drive Learning

Listen to what consumers say they want and work to give it to them. Then build a clever and effective marketing program around that product. With most projects, people start trying to learn first—determining the market, mapping out the likely competition, and then planning on how to live in that category. The only important reference point is the competition, whoever it might be. It is critical to remember that the most important reference point in building a campaign is the product or company itself. Nothing is more powerful than that kind of authenticity and the momentum it can generate. Again, be who you want to be, and compel others to see you in that way. Don't ask what they think. Instead, invite them in!

How do I look for ways to bring more of myself to my work? How do I keep defining myself? I walk the streets of Shanghai and Hong Kong and Tokyo, looking at people, looking in windows, looking at everything I can. I go into toy stores and robot stores and sneaker stores. I study graphic design and packaging in every country I visit. I go to Dai Nippon Printing in Japan to view next-generation packaging and sustainable materials and new types of ink. Instead of sitting in one place, anchored to what I already know, I am constantly learning and renewing myself. Insights are great. Foresight is better.

I try to draw from the legacy and history of marketing, as well. For example, I got in touch with James Ayers, one of the foremost American collectors of historic soft-drink bottles, and started buying up small collections of bottles, memorabilia, old advertising, signs, and just about everything I could get my hands on to create my own laboratory of culture: bottles and cans and fountains and signs and promotional materials and anything else that might give my company ideas. I wanted to be able to build a timeline of different bottling and packaging and marketing innovations over the years. I knew that if our work for the redesign of the Pepsi logo was grounded in bottler and design history, the new look would be much more potent and accurate.

Sometimes when you strive for simplicity, you wind up having people react as they do in the classic Hans Christian Andersen story "The Emperor's New Clothes." You come up with something very simple and people say, "What did you do?" or "You barely changed anything."

In the Andersen story, an emperor who loves new clothes is duped by two hustlers who say they will make him a special suit of clothing. The hustlers pretend to weave the cloth for the clothes but create nothing, telling the emperor that their "suit" is invisible to anyone who is stupid. Not wanting to appear stupid, the emperor and his entourage do not admit they see no clothing, and instead exclaim over how beautiful it is. When they are finished, the emperor dons the new "clothes!" During the procession, a child, innocent of others' expectations, calls out, "But the emperor has nothing on at all!"

Well, our goal is to design for people who are as honest and alert as that child, and not worry about any of the others, the followers. We ask ourselves, "How would an open-eyed child react?"

In our work to relaunch the Pepsi brand and design, we realized Pepsi's identity needed to be closer to expressing consumers' desires to have an experience with the brand. Peeling away the layers, excavating back through Pepsi's past, from the original flowing Victorian logos of 1898 to an ink-and-pen calligraphy look, we came as close as possible to the point of connection between the product and the consumer. In other words, we found the future of the company in the company's past. That was how we arrived at the smile, laugh, and grin, The three variations of the Pepsi logo.

Advertising Age recounted the story in October 2008 under the headline "Pepsi Upends Brands with $1.2 Billion Shake-up." The writer noted, "The white band in the middle of the logo will now loosely form a series of smiles. A smile will characterize brand Pepsi, while a grin is used for Diet Pepsi and a laugh is used for Diet Pepsi Max."

People love to discover something new. As a marketer, you can't really create a new trend, but you can jump on a trend's bandwagon. The enthusiastic public are who create trends, not marketers. It's much smarter to think instead of leading the market *to* a trend and capitalizing on that moment in time. There's nothing longer lasting, however, than intelligence and something well thought through.

In the case of Pepsi, we created an arrow pointing toward the future, a simple lift of the lip, an engaging smile, a recognition of the satisfaction that one gets from drinking Pepsi.

For me it was another case of the past and the present overlapping in a powerful way. Another reminder of how JFK's assassination, for example, helped to shape and mold me into the person I am. That is why I always try to hold on to pieces of the past, to its emotional truth, because those pieces and that truth can be guides to the future.

I always try to balance the world of documented references with the world of true creation. To balance respect for the past with the need to create a future without constraints.

The World at Your Fingertips

FORTY YEARS AGO, a young reporter named Joe McGinniss published a book called *The Selling of the President, 1968*, a shocking and brilliantly accurate glimpse of the future, as much as anything by George Orwell or Aldous Huxley or Alvin Toffler. McGinniss's essential insight was that, for all the romance and narrative power of Theodore White's "Making of the President" series, the cold, hard reality of politics was that candidates for president were increasingly being marketed the way household products like Colgate toothpaste or Tide laundry detergent were marketed.

Forty years later, our perspective on politics is wildly different. It turns out that even when you build an elaborate Astrodome of a construction, you can never control every bounce. It turns out that what smelled artificial and sinister to McGinniss—that early glimpse of the interconnected future—now looks exciting and energizing and far more empowering than anyone could have anticipated. It's not so much that technology has changed as that we have changed. Our BlackBerrys and Facebook profiles and YouTube contributions or downloads are just tools we use to express ourselves and connect with others, whether politicians or friends.

One of the remarkable aspects of the Barack Obama presidential campaign was that it was not about electing one man, even with all of history on the line; it was about tens of millions of people who had a chance to reinvent themselves through their experience of the political year. The Obama people found all kinds of new ways to get people involved, day in and day out, and keep them involved. You could drop by the Obama Web site and come home with enough widgets to keep you busy for days.

It really was bottom-up politics, rather than top-down as with the early eBay community. In short, it wasn't the ad men that Joe McGinniss worried about who created the images through which we viewed our politics; it was a new world in which we were creating these optics ourselves. And instead of looking cynical or calculating, it looks the opposite—fresh and open and democratic (small "d"). It has become a mass undertaking, a form of group art.

We have come a long way from the 1968 presidential election, when Richard Nixon defeated Hubert Humphrey. Nowadays no one objects to presidential contests being decided in large part by which candidate does a better job of projecting—and protecting—a vibrant and winning image. Presidential politics has in a sense become the ultimate competition in the ultimate national sport. I'm talking not only about politics but about the national sport of branding, of self-invention.

Political elections are a way of marking progress. People like Joe McGinniss in 1968 were disturbed by the social and cultural changes Richard Nixon was tapping into by using salesmanship. Now everyone uses those techniques. We see what works on the national stage, and it becomes more widely accepted. The Obama campaign was a perfect example of this process. It was a vehicle of change in a way that transcended the limits of past campaigns and shaped future campaigns—and our expectations about future campaigns—so dramatically that it will clearly be seen as a watershed.

In a sense the Obama campaign represented an explosion in our sense of the possible on the Internet; some call it the YouTube phenomenon. In the early days, YouTube was where you went to see homemade videos that others had put up there. Over time, YouTube became the place to see great video each of us had put up there. Even if you weren't actually putting up videos, you were encouraged to act on the assumption that one day you probably would. Right there, at the top of the page, just under the black-and-red-and-white YouTube logo, reads the banner "Broadcast Yourself."

Far from representing a threat to what people think of as the spirit of the 1960s, technology enhances that spirit of social change. It embodies the democratic values and attitudes of the 1960s by giving people new reach through the connectivity of the social media, via blogs, Facebook, YouTube, Twitter, MySpace, and others. It's popular history with a software upgrade. Positive, optimistic enthusiasts are tripping out on broadband rather than acid.

The quantum leap forward in technology that promotes connectivity, community, and sharing has profoundly shaped our culture and our attitudes, our passions and our habits. If Coke once taught the world to sing, today Coke would teach it how to remix. What started as information technology has turned into lifestyle technology that affects how we communicate and relate to one another. Yes, some PDAs sometimes get called "Crackberries" because of their addictive qualities, but the fact is technology is an amazing tool to help us achieve our goals and change our lives.

All of a sudden, through YouTube and Google and Facebook, people can finally express themselves to anyone on anything, from politics to sex to art to religion. With this neo-1960s populist revival, technology has as much impact as a march on Washington, with the ease and simplicity of a few keystrokes.

How quickly these new technologies have gone from conjecture to reality to cultural phenomena. Think of how much more change we are likely to live through in the years and decades ahead. Back in late 1945, the cartoonist Chester Gould paid a visit to the brilliant inventor Al Gross. From 1938 to 1941, Gross had developed—and patented—a "walkie-talkie" and presented it to Wild Bill Donovan, founder of the Office of Strategic Services (the forerunner of the CIA). Donovan put it to work in the U.S. military in World War II. After the war, Al Gross worked on developing a two-way wrist radio. During another visit, Gould was so impressed with what he saw that he introduced the idea into his *Dick Tracy* comic strip in January 1946 and made Dick Tracy a national hero with his two-way wrist radio (later a two-way wrist TV).

In the 1980s, long before BlackBerrys, iPhones, and cell phones, the gadget that had people talking was the pager. The early pagers—most people called them beepers—could only receive information. By 1990, 9.9 million pagers were in use in the United States, according to Economic and Management Consultants International, of Washington, D.C.

I remember my astonishment when the pager hit the market. We now had the capacity to communicate anywhere within seconds. I remember feeling unshackled. For me the step forward was all about subtraction: A layer of limitation had been removed, peeled away like the skin of an onion. Every remarkable step forward since then in technology and how we use it has stripped away more layers of limitation.

I love the idea that technology lets us speed up the processes of creation and reinvention. I love that through technology and the social media, we can brand ourselves, rebrand ourselves, and brand ourselves yet again. Technology is a living ecosystem. You can show it, tell it, and do it all over again. It gives people the power to broadcast who they are moment by moment. It makes yesterday seem, well, so yesterday.

CHAPTER 16

Reinvent the Obvious

ONE OF THE MORE SUBDUED, low-key pieces of design I helped to create in recent years is one that has made a wide impression: the HomeHero kitchen fire extinguisher, which I designed to sit on the kitchen counter. I took a 125-year-old product that had not evolved in years in aesthetics and user interface and gave it a much-needed face-lift. It finally moved from under the kitchen sink, tucked away somewhere behind the dishwashing liquid, to the countertop. The HomeHero is a good example of reinventing the obvious, making something more relevant for the times. Why did I decide to redesign the fire extinguisher? So it will not be taken for granted or ignored.

I have always been a fan of the Fire Department of New York. It's members are true heroes. Who else would run *into* a burning building to help save lives? When I started thinking about the heroism of the New York firefighters and their counterparts all over the country, I realized the importance of prevention, to lessen the likelihood of their having to run into fiery buildings. One of the first lines of defense in firefighting is what firefighters call a "can," a fire extinguisher carried and used by the "can man." A small kitchen fire can turn into a full-blown house fire in less than five minutes. If you can put out a kitchen fire with a fire extinguisher in those critical first few minutes, you can save your home, your life, and the lives of others.

I wanted to design a "can" that people could love so they would put it where they could grab it quickly. So I asked everyone in our office to take a photo of the fire extinguisher in her or his kitchen. The first surprise for me was how few of the people in my office knew where their fire extinguishers were. They had been out of sight for so long, unused (fortunately), that it took an effort for most of my employees to recall where they were. Then when the photos started coming in, I saw just what I expected: photos of fire extinguishers stashed under sinks, in cabinets, high on shelves, or in broom closets. These all-important devices were jammed behind mops, dust pans, food, soda, dishwashing liquid, and vacuum cleaners. They were hidden and hard to reach. Here was one of the greatest safeguards we can have in our homes, and almost no one among a group of hundreds of people valued them enough to keep them within easy reach.

That simple exercise, partnered with such authority as Tom Von Essen, former fire commissioner of the City of New York, and Lynn Tierney, former deputy fire commissioner of the City of New York, prompted me to design the HomeHero fire extinguisher. The fire extinguisher's basic look or functionality had not changed for about 125 years, which is why people hid it away. It was ugly. I wanted to design a fire extinguisher that was easier to use and had a stylish design so people would keep it on a countertop near the stove, ready to grab in case of fire. I designed a sleek, white canister with an easy, comfortable grip, clear visual instructions printed on the back, and superior, single-handed functionality. By reinventing the obvious, we took a century-old product and turned it into something stylish and beautiful and not likely to be taken for granted.

What we achieved with that fire extinguisher can be applied in our lives as well. Suppose you want to change the way people label and define you, to stop letting them take you for granted. You need to battle against complacency, against the ho-hum. HomeHero did this by adding a design element to promote visibility (so the extinguisher was not so ugly that it needed to be hidden away) and an easier grip and spray button (so it was not as intimidating to use). We reinvented the obvious. Why not reinvent the obvious in your life to give yourself more confidence and to effect change without forcing it?

Here are two examples of how to reinvent the obvious in your life:

- At your favorite restaurant, if you are on a diet, ask the owner or manager to reinvent the house special in a lower-calorie, lower-fat version for you.

- If you don't have time to go to the gym, reinvent what a workout means to you. Use light weights at home, stretch and do calisthenics, do a StairMaster-like routine on your second-floor or hallway or basement stairs. Walk around the block. You can reinvent your perspective on almost any issue if you are determined enough.

Concord is a luxury watch brand owned by Movado, the company that branded the "Museum Watch" with the plain face and singular dot at the top of the dial where "12" would be. Luxury-watch advertising has traditionally focused on precision, a superior movement, Swiss heritage, engineering, and quality of materials, such as gold and platinum. It has been all about being over the top. The luxury-watch category made a big deal about owning precision timepieces as a way to be in control of your life. It assumed that being in control of your time translated to being "on time."

Watch advertising typically showed the watch and a head shot of a celebrity endorser. Rolex photographed its watches in glamorous, out-of-the-way locations such as Hawaii. No Photoshop in Rolex ads. It was all about authenticity, to an absurd degree.

When Movado Group hired my company to create a new brand campaign for the Concord brand, we wanted to stand out from the crowd. The watch already had everything that its competition had, from precision movement and quality to celebrity endorsements and elegant, eye-catching style. So we decided to think differently. Instead of the same old same old, we focused on another part of the luxury-watch category: the customer. Instead of being all about the watch, we decided to showcase the lifestyle of the watch-wearer.

Our premise? If you could afford one of these watches, you also could probably afford to keep your own schedule and make decisions about how you spend your time. So we created an advertising campaign around a woman lying in bed, sleeping, covered by beautiful bed linens. On her arm was a Concord watch.

Our tagline? "Be Late." This was less a comment about the watch and its quality than it was a statement about the woman who was wearing the watch. This was an ad about her life, her ability to control her own time. The woman who was wearing this watch could afford to be late—for whatever event or reason.

The topics of "lateness" and "watches" had never been brought together before. If you were late, the watch was to blame, most people tended to think. Our advertising assumed that the watch was accurate and that the wearer chose to be late. It said: *Buy this watch, adopt this attitude, live this life.* It said: *Be seen beyond the context of the hardware on your wrist, and make a larger comment on your taste, style, and attitude.*

It's all about creating a new status quo. Giving people a new perspective from which to judge and assess a watch in their lives. By shifting the focus from the watch to the wearer, we treated the qualities of the watch as if they were assumed. It's similar to the Shift I went through when I went from heavy to thin. Although I was the same person, to others I went from "crazy and eccentric" to "energetic and stylish."

Each of us get labeled all the time. Let's say someone says of me, "Oh, there goes Peter, he's in advertising." It's such a small label; I've been so narrowly defined. I would much rather have people think, "Oh, there goes Peter, he does a million things: Advertising, design, he can solve many things for your brand."

Reinventing the obvious is about letting in some air and expanding others' perceptions. Some of this can be done through positioning: how you speak about yourself; what you write on your Facebook or LinkedIn page; how you compose an e-mail or a handwritten thank-you note. Some of it can be done through a "face-lift" of sorts: new look, hairstyle, clothes, glasses, accessories, or all of the above. Bring out your best self and minimize what you don't like that others may think about you. In our world, perception often is reality.

Part Two
Tactics That Work

CHAPTER 17

Find Your Mission

GET COMFORTABLE. I want to tell you the details of how I decided to reshape my life.

Specifically, think of yourself in a nice outdoor recliner. We're in my backyard. I've got a nice backyard at my house in Westchester, but like a lot of people with backyards, I don't give myself much time to kick back and enjoy it. I'm doing what I'd normally do on Memorial Day weekend. I'm sitting outside, next to a fountain on my back patio, calmly listening to the water and catching up on reading.

The Sunday magazine section has an article called "What's Doing In Rome." I'm always interested in what's doing in Rome, having spent so much time there. A piece in the Style section asks the question: "If Federico Fellini were alive and well today, would he go to fashion shows?"

One story that catches my eye is about the high rate of

heart attacks among overworked, overstressed, overweight men in my age group. I'd seen the statistics before, of course. I have heard this message many times over the years. There is no avoiding it. But this time it hits me differently. As I saw the kids playing nearby, smiling and laughing, it hits me, right to the center of me, how much my weight is impacting the probability that I will be sitting here again next fall. I could be dead by then, according to the article. It hits me how much I want to be around not only to see my kids, but to see *their* kids one day.

I weighed 406 pounds that day. I started doing the math and didn't like the cold logic of the numbers. If I was lucky—and if I was healthy—I could probably expect to see forty more summers of life, forty more summers of being with my family. But at 406 pounds, the last thing I wanted to think about was luck. Given my weight, I realized I wasn't likely to be lucky—unless I made some *major* changes.

We are who we love. We see ourselves in our love for others—our kids, our spouses and partners, our parents, our friends—and in their love for us. In my love for my family I suddenly had a brilliant and glimmering vision of myself—not as I was but as I *could* be. *Would* be, I decided. Once the vision had stung my eyes, I went from smiling to crying to laughing again in a rush. I looked out at my family and I knew. I could *see* what I was to become. I guess I was working my way back from the end result. But I took it as an absolute given that I was going to do this—I was going to lose all of that extra weight and live in the land of ambition and success. It was just a question of how to get from here to there.

Following that vision that afternoon, I was on a mission to transform myself. And it was the best kind of mission, one I had to undertake not only for me but for my family and my friends—above all for my grandfather, who I always knew was keeping an eye on me up there somewhere, winking at me now and then when I talked to a client or a friend about fishing where the fish are.

Transforming myself meant starting where we at Arnell always start with a new client, taking a long, close look at the brand—in this case, *my* brand. What did my weight say about me? What did it say about my brand? What did my signature loose-fitting khaki pants and billowing white shirts, always untucked, say about my image? How did my yo-yoing weight influence my brand recognition? Was I seen by others as reliable or as inconsistent? Was my obesity a factor in people's opinion of me? Was it a factor in people's view of my values?

I didn't have answers to all those questions at the moment, but merely raising them gave me a sinking feeling. But since I was looking at myself the way I would look at a new client, I was also excited. I always love the excitement of taking on a new project and turning around a brand. The bigger the challenge, the more exciting the project is.

The next step in my transformation involved creating a mission statement, just as I would craft for any branding campaign. Keep it simple and keep it true, I reminded myself: *My mission is not to lose weight—my mission is to have more time on earth. My mission is to elicit my true self.*

Next, I took my mission statement to some of the key Arnell executives. We put our heads together, as we do with any client, defining my new identity and visualizing success. From the beginning I decided on a mix of optimism and realism. I had to make smart choices about what would and would not work in terms of losing weight and keeping it off. I am almost always on a trip, or just back from a trip, or just about to make a trip. A lot of my trips take me halfway across the world. So I needed a branding program I could take with me wherever I traveled. It could not be overly dependent on my having face-to-face contact with doctors or advisers or any other people I was not likely to see for weeks at a time.

Here are the principles we consider basic to any successful branding campaign, which we decided to apply to me:

- Generate news and newness.
- Retain current audiences while expanding appeal.
- Translate the program on a global basis.
- Demonstrate superior differentiation.
- Revitalize brand image.
- Tap into pop culture for relevance.
- Live up to the brand promise on functional and emotional levels.

Envision yourself as a brand. A company doesn't take a brand off strategy to feel good or to indulge itself. After all, a brand has to be responsible to its constituencies to stay on message and be consistent. But a brand that is not moving forward is a brand that is moving backward. A brand that loses its dynamism risks going belly-up. That's why momentum and forward motion are so important in sustaining the brand that is you. I will explain in detail the different ways that you can ensure that you move forward and change your life.

The tactics I will be discussing are tools that everyone can master. Among the specific tactics I will explore for moving yourself forward are BE A TIGER, GO HELIUM, CREATE A FAN CLUB, SHOCK AND AWE, and EMBRACE MISTAKES. They show you what to do and what *not* to do. But before we can get to that, first you have to work on shearing away what is extraneous and unimportant in your life.

Branding is often about addition and multiplication. But it can also be about subtraction. We are constantly involved in personal struggles and campaigns—from finding a life partner to getting ahead at work, from saving money for a down payment on a house to caring for an elderly parent. Most of these are things few other people will ever hear about. That is why people love it when they get a chance to talk about their personal struggles. No matter where I am in my travels around the world, people love to talk about their personal struggles. I tell them I lost 256 pounds and changed things about myself as a person that were making me unhappy, and it's like a dam bursts. People describe in heartbreaking detail their own stories, and their hopes to overcome what holds them back; they voice their worry, their vulnerability, and their humanity. That catharsis is invaluable; that release is essential. You should build on it and amplify it.

CHAPTER 18

Un-write Your Life

DON'T WRITE THE STORY of your life. *Un*-write it. If that sounds backwards, that's just what you want: You should feel excited by this new perspective. Yes, the idea of un-writing flies in the face of everything we have been taught by our experiences in school, at work, and at home. We are told that if something is important, we should write it down. The 3M Post-it Note, which is part of the approximately $3 billion its division makes for 3M Company, is so successful because people equate writing something down with making a commitment to getting it done. You want to feel good about making a commitment to yourself, so you buy the colorful little squares or use the Stickies feature on your desktop. But how many of those tasks written down do you ever complete?

A commitment to change can start just as easily with a what-not-to-do list as with a to-do list. I believe you need to un-write your past in order to create the future of your choosing. Why? Fixing yourself in space and time with a rigid written agenda of what you plan to achieve and when you plan to achieve it does not allow for experimentation. It does not leave room for the adjustments you need to make as you begin to change your life. A written agenda that is inflexible and unforgiving is the antithesis of dynamic forward motion. To-do lists do not always clarify and simplify; instead, they can remove spontaneity, creativity, and joy. They can make you focus on the illusory goal of checking off the box and removing an item from the list, so that your actions become perfunctory instead of full of effort and sincerity.

So don't worry about the script or plotline. It's okay to make it up as you go along. If that means you make some mistakes, fine. You *want* to make mistakes. You *need* to make mistakes. You need to explore the feeling of cutting against the grain of the latest dogma and trusting your own hunch or intuition, no matter how it works out. And who is to say what is a mistake? I think Celine Dion is one of the greatest singers ever. One idea I worked on for Chrysler was a big campaign with Celine to cross-promote cars and her music. This to me was one of those rare organic moments where everything comes together. Celine was excited, and the TV spots were great. The commercials seemed to transport audiences with the message "Drive equals love." The plan even tested very well in the research it was put through. But for whatever reason, despite the positive consumer feedback, the campaign was not heralded in the press or by the trade to the degree Chrysler had expected. Had this entire effort been a mistake?

Some thought so. But ideas of "right" and "wrong" aren't always in the eye of the beholder. To me, the campaign was creativity in action and a total success. It fulfilled everything creatively I set out to achieve.

Every great idea can at times be seen by some as weird or wrong-headed. If the idea is really great, perhaps it will survive the doubts and prosper. Every marketer worth his or her salt has a story to tell of a great success that never would have happened without trusting a gut feeling and desire to try something new even in the face of withering doubt. The shoe that made Reebok a household name in 1982 was that kind of "mistake." Paul Fireman, the company's founder, was sent some shoe prototypes to check out. The soft leather at the toe was wrinkled. Paul was told the wrinkling was a glitch and he should ignore it. But he liked it. He wanted to make his shoes exactly like that. I'm sure some very high-powered marketing and design executives told Paul he was crazy. But he had un-written the part of him that got caught up in doubt, and he allowed himself to see something that others couldn't envision. He trusted his gut. The aerobics shoe was an instant hit that soon became a 1980s fashion statement.

By the time Reebok asked my company to start working with them, twenty years later, the brand was struggling. The company's wrinkly-tipped women's aerobic shoe was so successful that it actually became the image of the company. Reebok was at risk of being seen as "my mother's" or "my sister's" brand by the key sneaker-buying audience, which consisted mostly of fifteen-year-old males. After a business and budget assessment, we decided to create a new sub-brand that would come from the core of Reebok heritage but be especially designed for the young male audience. We wanted to give members of this audience something new that they could immediately relate to, rather than trying to convince them that Reebok was cool enough, again, to be their sneaker of choice. That would have taken too much time and money. We needed to get this customer back into the Reebok brand another way.

Reeboks began as a running shoe from England. The company was founded late in the nineteenth century as J. W. Foster and Sons and renamed itself Reebok in 1958, using the South African spelling for an animal resembling a gazelle. The shoe was known for being lightweight and designed for speed, like a gazelle. We decided speed should connote the essence of the new brand—but speed in a new, modern, aspirational way likely to resonate with urban trend-buying teens and young adults.

So we looked at the essence of speed and power from another angle. We looked at slang—the language youth use to communicate with one another—and we saw that increasingly it consisted of shorthand references. Then we looked at the stock ticker and saw that the ticker symbol for Reebok was "rbk." That was it—three letters that said Reebok but without any vowels. Short and sweet. And the three letters symbolized money, energy, and success. This essence of the brand was now going to be made relevant for today. Rbk was created. And to continue to provide youth with the currency they want, we decided to hire not only sports stars, as sneaker brands do, but also music stars. We worked with Jay-Z and the Rbk design team in Boston; Shawn Carter, the brand we created with him for Rbk, hit the streets as successfully as Nike's Air Jordan. Then we did a series of spots featuring a character called Terry Tate, Office Linebacker. They were short, comedic sketches of Terry tackling his coworkers for such offenses as taking the last cup of coffee in the pot and not making more. The brand had its attitude back.

Un-writing can help you to create the story you want to tell, rather than the one you think you have to tell. So when you sit down to un-write your story, create a story line about yourself that you want to perpetuate. Build it into your strategic brand-building program. Wire it into your personal DNA. It should carry the energy and excitement of the ongoing change you want to make in your life. Like DNA, it needs to be coded in a way that is simple and strong and won't unravel at the first hint of challenge or trouble. You need to be guided by the story line that you built for yourself. And once you start forward, you want to keep moving forward along your path without a lot of stops and starts. Adjustments are a given. You can't foresee every circumstance or how you will respond to the unexpected. Don't worry about that. Challenge yourself with long-term goals. Be sure you have a story line you can make work for you; then start down your new path without thinking too much about its curves and dips.

Here's my story line: I had a reputation for being extreme. People expected me to act a certain way in every meeting, running around, getting all worked up, and screaming out what I was feeling. At 406 pounds it was easy to get all worked up. I would sweat profusely just walking up a flight of stairs, let alone putting on a board-room display. Because I was so heavy, I wore elastic-waisted khaki pants, Air Force One sneakers, and white, buttoned-down shirts, always untucked. So when my arms flew up in the air in a meeting—which was often—my shirt would fly up, baring my stomach to all in the room.

Needless to say my meetings were always fun and full of energy, jokes, and loud sounds. My whole presentation was a spectacle. I designed my look and developed my persona to try to make my obese self appear energetic and healthy, to make me seem like just another eccentric creative type. That image, however, could not have been farther from the truth. My ankles always hurt because they had so much strain on them. I had a bad back. As for my energy—sure, I was amped up, but I was drinking espresso every hour on the hour.

This kind of false performance couldn't go on forever, and I knew it. I got tired of being introduced by friend and colleagues as some kind of eccentric, especially as my company added as clients some conservative packaged-good businesses.

"This Peter," they would say, "he's a genius, but he's crazy! Watch who you put in a meeting with him because he'll be running around the room with his billowy white shirt flapping up around his head at some point! But you will get brilliant ideas from him."

My story or image cut both ways. But I realized that the crazy-Peter part was starting to overshadow my good work. I had created a myth about myself—about the way I wanted myself to be perceived—as an implicit defense against anyone who was put off by my extreme weight. But as the myth took on its own momentum, it began to backfire. Then as my waist-line shrank, I needed to discover my new myth, a new story, in which people would see my intense approach to work balanced by an extreme sense of calm and ease with myself.

My new image was not without drawbacks. Calm is good; too much serenity is not. If you are too calm, you can fade into the woodwork. I did not want perceptions of me to flip from one extreme to the other, from "over the top" to someone "without a pulse." I wanted an evolution of my story that would keep all the good parts of being high-energy and creative without the baggage of my former eccentricity and high-energy behavior. I decided to create a new story line for myself early on, instead of waiting for others to create one for me.

I wanted to maintain the energy and excitement and passion I brought to the table and put it in a new-and-improved package. This was the same dynamic I brought to my work designing new bottles for SoBe Lifewater. A fun, expectation-defying bottle cannot make the beverage inside taste better, but if the beverage does taste better, a new look can help a consumer notice—and remember. A new look, backed up with substantive change, can help shift perceptions.

Today I am thin. I am calmer. I have long since abandoned my old uniform of loose white shirts and khaki pants. I wear fitted suits as appropriate for a business executive and the chief creative officer of my company and the chief innovation officer to countless other companies. I tuck in my shirts. Now when I run around the room during a meeting—you didn't expect me to give *that* up, did you?—my buttoned-down look helps balance out my effusive style. My look and my style reinforce each other. I am still the same person. I still work hard to deliver superior work. I like to think that my meetings are still fun. My personal rebranding, however, has given my audience a new perspective on who I am and what I have to offer.

Today, I believe people see me for who I am. They don't get sidetracked reacting to my weight or to the eccentric-Peter persona I needed before. At some point it may be time to shift my story line again, if I am going to continue along the path of change, growth, and improvement. I may once again have to un-write my story and my brand. But now is not that time. I am living the life that I wanted to live. I am fulfilling the desires and dreams I had for myself when I sat on my patio that day, watching my kids play.

If I can do it, you can, too. Stop locking yourself into start-and-stop dates and unrealistic goals. That's a trap, like annual New Year's resolutions. Personal transformation is a long-term evolution, one that you can't always control with a rigid, artificial time frame. Pay attention to your feelings. Don't be afraid to make mistakes. A mistake might turn out to be the best thing that can happen to you. It might turn out to be precisely what you need to make a breakthrough. In fact, remove the word *mistake* from your vocabulary and un-write it as a new way to define *opportunity*.

CHAPTER 19

Be a Tiger

JACK KEROUAC, the sad, cool, genius from Lowell, Massachusetts, wrote a novel about the power of self-invention called *On the Road*. That might not be the idea most people have about Kerouac's famous book, but believe me, it's the real subject. Kerouac's characters are forever dreaming of finding some other, better versions of themselves waiting to be claimed in this or that far-off place, if only they can drive or hitch or ride to where they need to go. San Francisco? New York? Mexico? The specific destination hardly matters. The genius of Kerouac is his insight that it's not all about the getting there, it's not even about making the most of your journey underway. It's about leaving parts of yourself behind, leaving old stories about yourself behind, leaving old ideas about yourself behind. In short, it's about *un*-writing your life.

Of all the things you need to leave behind, though, none

ranks quite as high as worry. At one point in the book, Dean Moriarty says, "Now you just dig them in front. They have worries, they're counting the miles, they're thinking about where to sleep tonight, how much money for gas, the weather, how they'll get there—and all the time they'll get there anyway, you see. But they need to worry and betray time with urgencies false and otherwise, purely anxious and whiny, their souls really won't be at peace unless they can latch on to an established and proven worry and having once found it they assume facial expressions to fit and go with it, which is, you see, unhappiness, and all the time it all flies by them and they know it and that *too* worries them no end."

We flatter ourselves with the idea that the burdens we insist on carrying are unique and original; but, really, nothing is less unique or original. Montaigne observed in his *Essays 1512,* "He who fears he shall suffer, already suffers what he fears."

Ralph Waldo Emerson, the great American Transcendentalist, picked up the theme more than 250 years later. "It is never worth while to worry people with your contritions," Emerson wrote in his journal in late 1841. "We shed our follies and absurdities as fast as the rose-bugs drop off in July and leave the apple tree which they so threatened. Nothing dies so fast as a fault and the memory of a fault. I am awkward, sour, saturnine, lumpish, pedantic and thoroughly disagreeable and oppressive to the people around me. Yet if I am born to write a few good sentences or verses, those shall endure and my disgraces utterly perish out of memory."

I'd have loved to work with Ralph Waldo. I've got a bag

full of approaches one can use to try to turn your back on worry. I'd have loved to show them to Ralph Waldo. I have a whole passel of approaches that can help you, which I sum up with fun names like "Be a Tiger" and "Go Helium." All of them start with an understanding of this line by Toni Morrison: "Wanna fly, you got to give up the shit that weights you down."

To most people Chris Rock is a funny guy from the Bed-Stuy section of Brooklyn. To me Chris is a wise man and a lifestyle guru. Does the idea shock you? Good. But think about it: Chris is quick, smart, topical, in tune with cultural movements, and very, very, very funny. What are most good jokes? Exercises in un-writing. We laugh and we strip away tired ways of seeing something. The freshness of what is revealed is stimulating and exciting; we feel like laughing.

Some of the best advice Chris ever gave came in a wild stand-up routine he did after everyone was talking about the famous event in 2003 when the Vegas act Siegfried & Roy took a tragic turn. Montecore, a 600-pound white Siberian tiger, bit trainer Roy Horn and dragged him away, almost killing him. The tiger had been obedient through six and a half years of shows—"six days a week, 45 weeks a year," as the *New York Times* noted. Until the Friday night in question.

"The tiger bit the man in the head, and everyone's mad at the tiger," Chris Rock said onstage. "Talk about the tiger went crazy."

Chris was right, too. That's what everyone had been talking about at the time.

"That tiger ain't go crazy," Chris continued. "That tiger went *tiger*!"

What a great phrase—the tiger went tiger!

"You know when the tiger went *crazy*?" Rock asked. "When the tiger was riding around on a little bike with a Hitler helmet on. 'Oh, shit. I'm a crazy tiger. Oh, Lord. I'm crazy. What is I goin' do?'"

Right after I heard that routine, I had the phrase "The Tiger Went Tiger" printed up large and mounted on the wall near the main entrance of the Arnell offices in Manhattan.

Why did a zinger from a Chris Rock comedy routine become my mantra for change? Because what he said was so true. It made me wonder where else that same thinking applied. It occurred to me that so many things we assume to be one way in life might be just as wildly off, just as cut off from their true nature as that 600-pound white Siberian tiger riding around on a bike.

We all get stuck in roles that aren't really us. We're desperate to break away, to break loose, but something keeps us toiling away even if it feels all wrong. Well, Chris Rock was right. If it feels all wrong, it probably is. Ultimately, we have to revert to our true natures. We have to ignore the people waving at us to do something their way. We have to leap to our destinies and be who we are. We have to *go tiger*.

Let me explain how this process works: One challenge of my personal rebranding campaign was handling the obvious danger of falling back into old bad habits. So much of my work requires me to be out at dinners and receptions and parties and you-name-it. Often at these functions perfectly well-meaning people come up to me and offer me all the wrong kinds of food. I know better. If I ate that food, I would be violating my program, my mission, and my strategy. For a time, though, I gave in here and there and ate what they offered me. I had any number of rationalizations for eating that stuffed mushroom or mini hamburger:

It was polite.
It was all there was.
Everyone else was.
I had only one.
I had no choice.
It was the easiest thing to do.
I didn't want to be any trouble.
I didn't want to call attention to myself.
I was good yesterday.
I'll be good tomorrow.

The subject here is not food. The subject here is not weight loss or weight gain. The subject here is what we must do to achieve the kind of sweeping personal change that can make a profound difference in our lives. I bet you recognize some of the excuses listed above. Have words like those, ideas like those, helped you rationalize acting against your own deeper wishes and best interests? If so, then you need to be a tiger. Being a tiger means that you need to focus on yourself and only on yourself when it comes to your core mission—in my case, my health and well-being. It means channeling your inner animal and not letting anyone or anything stop you from being who you know you can be.

It's about reclaiming the initiative. I went tiger before my older daughter's junior-high-school graduation, rather than resorting to any of the aforementioned excuses. I brought my own dinner and pulled it out during the banquet following the ceremony. Everyone else was eating chicken or filet, and I was happily chomping away on radishes, flavored seaweed crisps, cherry tomatoes, and grilled vegetables. I was surrounded mostly by teachers and other parents I had never met, and of course everyone asked about my food. I explained I was on a mission, and they understood. The teachers and other parents were very supportive. People respect a person on a mission. I went tiger that night by planning what would be best for me, even if it meant making special arrangements. And guess what? It wasn't at all embarrassing. In fact, it was nothing less than liberating.

I was able to go tiger in the workplace, too. That's what I did in 1996 when I was hired by Samsung to rebrand the Korean electronics giant. The work was strongly unconventional, so unusual that it was as if we were throwing everything out the window and starting all over. It went against category norms, traditional marketing, and traditional media.

We were looking to make a statement about Samsung, to relaunch the brand with a fresh campaign that would give people the feeling of confidence along with a high level of superior differentiation. But to do so, we decided to pick and focus on one product, and we chose the microwave oven.

Why? First of all, the microwave had a good reputation for functionality, and we were sure we could leverage that. Also, we wanted to build on Samsung's reputation with a key, timely piece of information we had recently seen some findings on: Fresh vegetables cooked in microwaves maintain far more of their nutrients than vegetables that are boiled or steamed through conventional means.

Here is the essence of what we wanted to target: In the mid-1990s, the microwave was new and sexy. We wanted to position the Samsung microwave as a critical accessory that everyone interested in pursuing a healthy lifestyle had to have. It's hard to remember now, but at first people tended to view the microwave as a mere convenience. It was used mostly to boil a little water for tea or heat a TV dinner. People did not associate it with healthy living. Most microwave ads showed frantic domestic scenes with the microwave looming on the kitchen counter as a busy mom returned home from work and popped in a frozen pizza for the kids' dinner. There was nothing wrong with that association—microwaves *are* convenient. But the message had become overly familiar and unexciting. It was timid and boring.

We had to crack that conventional message open and strongly link it to the Samsung brand. We had to un-write the assumptions behind the microwave's message, just as we had to crack open the notion that operating a microwave—using a strange form of radiation that many of us had never heard of—was somehow inherently unhealthy. Or the idea that the preparation of healthy food required a certain amount of time and effort and drudgery. Food that was prepared fast, it was widely thought, was bad for you. Veggies needed time and tender loving care and would not benefit from being slapped into a microwavable dish and zapped for four minutes.

To convey our new message about the healthful benefits of the Samsung microwave, we needed to go tiger. We came up with Microwave Man, a young bodybuilder with a beautiful, sculpted body. We placed a microwave oven under his muscular, outstretched arm and let the world see his sleek, toned, fit chest and washboard stomach as he carried the microwave out of the store with the phrase "Simply Samsung." His superfit chest and shoulders gave people the necessary link: Sexy and microwaves go together. Healthy living and fitness and microwaves go together.

To make a big first impression with the Microwave Man icon, we found a great building front in Manhattan, right across from a thriving Chelsea flea market, and put up a forty-feet-high by sixty-feet-wide picture of Microwave Man, the largest wall hanging anywhere at the time. And soon everyone was talking about him. Our going tiger with the Microwave Man campaign was a huge success and helped to reinvigorate Samsung. The story of the Samsung microwave's success showcases the point that a brand name really matters; that it has real meaning and value and can command a higher price in the marketplace. The same microwave from GE, for example, which was made in the same factory, to the same specifications, did not end up having the same value as the Samsung microwave after the Samsung brand name was given refreshed meaning and relevance to consumers.

Being a tiger means not caring if people think you're a

little crazy. It means doing what feels right to you, based on your knowledge of a situation, your desires and goals, and your instincts. Being a tiger means getting out of your rut or off your treadmill and doing what's in your nature, what you know you need to do to help yourself, your family, and your friends.

So if you are embarking on a major personal change—whether your goal is to quit smoking, get more fit, or reinvent your approach to your work, life, and career—you need to hear a compliment when people tell you "You're crazy!" Their comment means you're successfully going tiger. It means you're finding the inner focus you need to keep from wavering from the mission at hand. It means *you* are being *you*—clear, focused, concentrated, and powerful.

Go Helium

THE BEST WAY to deal with worry is to tackle it straight on. When you try to push your concerns away, they only become a distraction. If you embrace your concerns, you can let the inevitable fear float up and away and be done with it! You can, in short, do what the late great Los Angeles–based psychiatrist Milton Wexler recommended: Go helium.

A great man and friend, Milton was a remarkable person by any measure. Born in San Francisco and raised in New York, he initially studied law but went back to school to master psychiatry and eventually moved to Southern California and established a very successful practice. Marilyn Monroe was one of his patients, as was the director Blake Edwards. Blake and Milton were so close, their creative impulses were so intertwined, that Blake gave Milton screenwriting credits on two of his movies, *The Man Who Loved Woman* and

That's Life. Milton died of pneumonia in 2007 at the age of ninety-eight. As extraordinary as his life was, his obituary focused on his remarkable contributions to fighting Huntington's disease, a rare genetic disorder.

Milton's research found the genetic marker for Huntington's disease in 1983, and ten years later, Milton identified the gene. David E. Housman, an MIT biology professor, told the *New York Times* that the research set in motion by Milton's work "changed everything in the world of genetic disease."

I used to see Milton often when I was in L.A. I was introduced to him by my friend Frank Gehry. No one had a better strategy for tackling worry head-on, or a better way to do that: by going helium. To Milton, helium was the answer to everything. It takes you to a higher level. When you breathe it in, it changes—suddenly and completely—how you sound. It's the perfect antidote to worry. No wonder it's so much fun to untie a balloon and inhale the gas inside!

Helium is a natural gas lighter than air. In fact, it's the second lightest element, after hydrogen, and also the second most abundant element in the universe. But unlike hydrogen, which is famously flammable and volatile, helium is inert—it is neither volatile nor flammable. If you've seen footage of the German airship *Hindenburg* erupting in flames over a New Jersey naval air station in 1937 and plunging to its destruction, you know the dangers of using hydrogen gas.

So although hydrogen and helium both have lift, helium is one of the least reactive of all elements. It does not react with other elements even as it transports you. "Going helium" means to rise up and float freely, rising above your problems and concerns, going as high as you can go. Going helium is about capturing a feeling of freedom within yourself to go farther than you thought you could. Milton constantly talked about how people set their goals too low. Fear and worry make them focus on trying to guard against failure, rather than focusing on success. Helium is the enemy of such fear and concern. Helium pushes us up, with few discernible drawbacks.

People or brands that go helium go beyond the obvious. They look for greater benefits, which are often the most difficult to identify because they require vision and leaps of faith. Nothing I've worked on better fits that description than the Peapod, the all-electric car I developed for Chrysler. This is the ultimate brand creation story, about developing a product created not merely to satisfy consumer needs but to help make a better world. From the beginning of this project, we truly had a higher mission in mind—that is, going helium, with the whole world watching.

Peapod is a slow road, all-electric car that was born at Chrysler in 2008. (Intended as an urban transport vehicle, it is legal on all streets and roads with speed limits of 30 miles per hour or less.) There has been talk about electric cars in Detroit for years, and every major car manufacturer has an electric car in development. But the reality of mass-producing affordable electric cars is years away, although the need is immediate. The developmental thinking on the Peapod did not stop at decreasing carbon footprints and increasing fuel efficiency. We looked at every aspect of design and manufacturing with an eye toward improving the planet.

Chrysler is the owner of a small brand called GEM, short for Green Eco Mobility; it quietly established itself as the number-one electric vehicle brand in the United States. GEM vehicles usually are not typically sold to consumers. They are purchased by corporations with large campuses, by parks departments, and by many other businesses and organizations that need small, efficient vehicles to transport people within large, confined areas. GEM has been in existence for ten years and has a proven platform. It was Bob Nardelli, then chairman of Chrysler, who had the foresight to use the existing GEM platform to accelerate development time and tap into this big piece of "green" expertise and success already within the company.

Using the GEM platform, I began to put together my dream of what eventually became the Peapod. Not the actual design, but the dream. The Peapod took its inspiration from an actual peapod. What is more natural and beautifully designed than a peapod that carries and protects the peas inside? The Peapod vehicle was intended to be a natural container for "peas" or, in this case, people. It was designed for the average person, the individual consumer, rather than a corporate fleet buyer. The Peapod needed to address multiple environmental issues, including energy conservation, recyclability, materials and manufacturing, as well as carbon footprints and cost savings. The Peapod needed to be thought of as a self-contained environment that would ensure comfort, body ergonomics, quality of experience, and driver confidence.

With the dream defined, I began designing the vehicle, reinventing all the steps and processes that go into car design.

When we were all done, we gave the Peapod a front grille that almost makes the car look like it is smiling. We had designed a happy vehicle, in response to what the world needs in a car. And that, I feel, is something to smile about.

The Peapod is made entirely from recycled and recyclable materials. We created special seats, more like office chairs than car seats, to provide lumbar support and superior comfort. We made the vehicle easy to recharge, by plugging it in as you would your cell phone, and it's just about as cheap to recharge. We gave it consumer-friendly features such as a removable roof for good-weather driving and enough roominess that even a six-foot-eight man can sit in it without drawing his knees up to his chin. Peapod is my version of going helium.

Going helium is not about reaching for the status quo, but about creating a new status quo that goes beyond others' imaginations. Once you go helium, you will realize that people have been waiting for you to do exactly that.

For a recent birthday, Milton gave me an unusual present: a bundle of forty-eight one-dollar bills. He told me to burn one bill every year on my birthday in a small ceremony. The purpose of this ritual is to remind myself every year I have one less year of life remaining. It is a reminder to focus more intently on my goals and mission to continue to change and grow. Aging should not be equated with slowing down, Milton told me. It should motivate us to *get going*. To reach even higher. To go helium. *Failure*, he said, is not reaching for something and falling short; it's not reaching high enough and not falling at all.

When I went to see Dr. Louis Aronne, an expert on obesity and the director of the Comprehensive Weight Control Program at New York–Presbyterian Hospital/Weill Cornell Medical Center in New York, I weighed 406 pounds. He knew how busy I was, and he knew that I probably would not return. So he created a program for me by e-mail.

On that first visit Dr. Aronne told me that if I could drop my weight from 406 pounds down to 230 pounds, he could work on the arithmetical problem I had been struggling with since that weekend when I sat in my backyard in Westchester, watching my children. Dr. Aronne told me that if he and I were able to get me down to a weight of 230 pounds, the math would no longer be against me. At that weight, I could count on living out my natural life span. If I could do that, he said, he'd keep me alive until my natural time came.

That was a nice enough goal. But I realized it wasn't nearly enough, and that's why Dr. Aronne and I decided to go helium. Forget about achieving a very challenging goal like getting down to 230 pounds! What would be an *ideal* goal? What would be the goal if we broke through all the barriers of old habits and self-limitation? 180 pounds? That sounded crazy—always a good thing!—dropping down to 180 pounds when I was at 406. But that was what I did. I'm sure Dr. Aronne never in a million years believed I would get there. The failure rate of people like me is very high. But I'd decided to go helium. Being crazy wasn't enough. So Dr. Aronne and I talked about taking me all the way down to 150 pounds. That was my goal. What would that represent to me?

If I went from 406 to 230 pounds, there was no question

the world would notice. People would think of me as a walking miracle, a man who had lost more than 180 pounds. But most would still see me as heavy, because 230 pounds at five-feet-eight would still seem large. Even if I lowered my weight all the way to 180 pounds, I would still be seen as somewhat chubby. And that perception would remain part of my brand: Peter Arnell, creative visionary and chubby man. But if I were able to get down to 150 pounds, I would look great and I would feel great. I would be seen as thin, fit, and healthy—three adjectives that would give me an enormous boost of confidence and strengthen my brand with my colleagues, clients, and friends. This is how helium works: It lifts you up and allows you to reach your proper altitude. My helium was helping me to bring my weight down while lifting my altitude and attitude up.

When you go helium, you laugh at the idea of failure. Unimaginable success doesn't seem unimaginable anymore. If I had dropped my weight down to 180 pounds—an astonishing 226-pound weight loss—Dr. Aronne would have been thrilled. I would have been happy, too. But I would not have felt that rush and sense of pure joy, that whoosh of helium, that thrill of going beyond the impossible. Today, at under 150 pounds, I am still floating on helium. It gives me the charged feeling of vaulting beyond the possible every single day, and the immense energy and satisfaction that go along with that accomplishment.

President John F. Kennedy understood helium. Plenty of people thought Kennedy was crazy when he started talking early in his presidency about a goal so bold and dramatic that it boggled the imagination. "I believe that this nation should commit itself to achieving the goal, before this decade is out, of landing a man on the moon, and returning him safely to the Earth," Kennedy told a joint session of Congress on May 25, 1961, speaking less than three weeks after astronaut Alan Shepard became the first American in space. "No single project will be more impressive to mankind, or more important in the long-rang exploration of space; and none will be so difficult or expensive to accomplish."

Wow—that is going helium in a big way! Not everyone was instantly sold on the idea. But the young president knew it was an aggressive goal that would help to unite the nation. Even before he was sworn in, the president-elect was worried about falling behind in the space race with the Soviet Union. A task force warned John F. Kennedy that the United States lagged behind the Soviet Union in ballistic missiles and outer-space exploration, according to the *New York Times*. Even before beginning his presidential campaign, Kennedy had felt "we ought to spend the money, the time and the effort to surpass the Russian effort."

Feeling a sense of urgency, Kennedy went helium, and he wanted the whole country to go helium with him. In a speech at Rice University in 1962 he said, "We choose to go to the moon in this decade and do the other things, not because they are easy, but because they are hard, because that goal will serve to organize and measure the best of our energies and skills."

To me, John F. Kennedy is a first-ballot inductee into the Helium Hall of Fame. Six years after Kennedy's tragic death in Dallas, Neil Armstrong took one small step for a man and one giant leap for mankind. Talking with me at a Special Olympics event, Kennedy's sister Eunice Kennedy Shriver offered me a tribute that I'm not sure I'd earned but I will never forget: "My brother Jack would have loved you. He always admired people whose feet never touch the ground."

That's how I would like all of us to be.

And the way to do it is by going helium. Thanks, Milton.

Create a Fan Club

SOME OF WHAT I SAY can sound self-contradictory. And sometimes it *is*. But Ralph Waldo Emerson, in his essay "Self-Reliance," warned, "A foolish consistency is the hobgoblin of little minds, adored by little statesmen and philosophers and divines." My point? As you go tiger or go helium, you have to be both flexible and inflexible. You have to start with a keen awareness of how others see you, on the one hand, and you have to stop worrying about how they see you, on the other hand. Nevertheless, you can't pretend you don't care what people think of you. We all care. We're human.

That's why achieving our mission has to be a team undertaking. We need help in marking our progress forward and in warding off the dangers of descending into the land of mumbo jumbo and murkiness, where we can convince ourselves of anything. That's why I believe in creating a fan club to cheer me along and keep me honest. Plenty of people have fan clubs who don't deserve them nearly as much as you do. We *all* deserve a fan club. So what if we have to put it together ourselves?

Creating my own fan club was a way to keep myself on track. For years I had been disappointing people. My clients had given up on having healthy food at meetings because it was invisible to me as I chowed down on the towering pastrami-on-rye I'd ordered from Katz's Deli on Houston Street. I had let my friends down so much that they didn't even bother to ask me how my alleged diet of the moment was going. So many times, I had promised my kids I would lose weight and then never lived up to my promise. So many times, I had let myself down.

The truth is, it's especially easy to disappoint the people who love us, because we know they love us and therefore will always try to find ways to forgive us. I knew I needed to build a trip wire of consequences into my mission if I was going to succeed. I wanted a crowd of energetic, positive, but open-eyed people involved in my mission. So I created a Peter Arnell Fan Club to encourage and support my efforts. And I made sure to broadcast my first early success—dropping below 400 pounds—far and wide. I did the same with the many other successes that followed.

If you broadcast your watershed moments to an extended group of friends and other well-wishers, you quickly reach a point of no return. Backsliding becomes out of the question, because disappointing so many people would be too painful. I knew full well that I could never ask so many people to forgive me or give me another chance. The members of your fan club will get bored quickly if you stop making progress. They expect to hear exciting, encouraging developments from you that they can pass on.

Today's new technology can be such an asset in creating and maintaining a fan club. You can send out regular e-mails, keeping your fans posted about your trip to the tailor to have your entire wardrobe resized, or describing the sensation you created at an annual meeting in Osaka or Ontario or Ojai when you showed up 100 pounds lighter than you had been at the same meeting a year earlier. You can start your own blog, where members of your fan club can stop by for updates, pictures, videos, or whatever you want to leave for them there. And of course, they can leave posts for you, offering their support and encouragement or challenging you to reach some bold new goal. The social networking sites offer another tool to connect with like-minded people and build a community—giving others a stake in your success and your mission.

Today, you can make the world your brand consultant and image manager. Why not capitalize on the goodwill and advice of all those people sitting by their computers ready to have their say? That is the beauty of the technologically interconnected, socially networked life. You want privacy? Fine—just turn off your cell phone or put your BlackBerry on "silent." It's your choice. Need a little feedback or inspiration? Send out a group e-mail to your friends-and-family list, and then sit back and read all the replies that come in. Don't like or disagree with what you read? Hit "delete."

In my line of work, consumer branding, we focus on the

need not just to have customers *buy* a product but to *join* a brand. It is a topic that comes up every single day. We need to issue an *invitation*, not push for a *transaction*. We need to turn our audience into our fans.

The same is true of us as individuals.

My company took exactly this approach to Hanes hosiery in 1996. We realized the old ways of advertising women's hosiery were no longer going to work. People wanted more information than "Silky!" or "Run-resistant!" or "Available in 12 different skin-tone shades!" Because women were dressing more casually in the workplace, they were less likely to wear—and buy—hosiery. The way to leverage that change was to turn it into an asset. We needed to inspire women to connect with hosiery on an emotional level once again; we needed fans, not consumers. The message we came up with was that hosiery had staying power as a stylish fixture of the fashion landscape.

We were very lucky in our choice of a messenger: Tina Turner, a woman famous for much, much more than her great legs. She was the queen of rock and roll with, at last count, eight Grammy Awards. She was a legendary dancer and singer who held her own as an actress, as well. Tina had been a fashion icon for years. In her fifties, Tina was still one of the sexiest women in the world. Everything about her was upbeat and inspiring.

She was not simply a survivor. She was a monument to the struggle and change needed in order to live a successful, happy life. Most people knew some of the details of her difficult marriage to Ike Turner. They knew she had come through a lot of hardship. Nonetheless, in her singing and in her presence onstage she glowed with a love of life. Even before we debuted the Hanes hosiery ad campaign, reaction in the press was phenomenal.

"The owner of what may well be the most glamorous gams since Betty Grable's is the star of an elaborate cross-marketing effort to promote Hanes hosiery," the *New York Times* breathlessly reported.

The brand we were marketing, Resilience, was a perfect fit for Tina. In the thirty-second TV spot, she told her millions of fans, "Resilience: It's all about strength and beauty." Tina looked great, of course, but she also came across as real, authentic, and approachable. She was brilliant. The feedback we got on the spot was unprecedented. Women who saw the commercial decided they were going to stand up for Hanes and its positive message for women. Some said it was personally inspiring and reminded them to fight for what they wanted in life. And that body-hugging bit of spandex that smoothed women's legs became the symbol for much, much more.

We started something of a movement with those ads. Oprah Winfrey took her talk show on the road with Tina for a week, doing shows devoted to praising resilient women who struggle to make a better life for their families, who struggle to make their dreams come true. Oprah loved Tina, and audiences did, too.

At one point during the tour, Oprah said, "I've been wearing Hanes every day and I still don't have legs like Tina."

The women loved it all. Sales of Hanes hosiery benefited from all this attention. And everyone had a great time. Oprah joined Tina onstage for a concert at the Greek Theater in Los Angeles, singing and dancing with her, and seemed to be having the time of her life accompanying Tina in a performance of Tina's signature hit "Simply the Best."

"I'm still on a high," Oprah later said on her show.

We had created the ultimate fan club, a mutual admiration society starring Tina Turner, with all her glamour and strength and beauty. Everyone identified with Hanes for recognizing the daily struggles of working women and single moms. It became more than a brand—it became a cause.

Oprah has always understood the importance of having a vocal, supportive, but not blindly uncritical fan club. And she has always understood that the only way to get that kind of support and fan club is to ask. The great Leonardo da Vinci, one of my heroes, realized that, as well. A master painter and sculptor, Leonardo was also a brilliant inventor, mathematician and engineer, musician and writer. One of the ways he became so successful was by going helium, going tiger, and creating his own fan club.

If you go to the Louvre in Paris and stand near the *Mona Lisa*, the first thing that will hit you is the mob scene there. I used to visit the Louvre on quiet afternoons off-season and have time alone to study the inscrutable wonder of that portrait. Not anymore: Leonardo's portrait may be the most famous painting in the world. Yet the thirty-year-old artist had to pitch his services to the duke of Milan, Ludovico Sforza, laying out in considerable detail in a letter what he had to offer.

The duke never answered Leonardo's letter, but he hired

the artist and kept him employed for the next sixteen years. I mention the letter because it represents an important lesson. If a genius like Leonardo couldn't get what he wanted without asking for it, why should you or I expect anything less? Leonardo was not an arrogant self-promoter. He also was not particularly sought after. So, like the rest of us, he had to pitch new business. The next time you have to apply for something—and, of course, while you're creating your own fan club—think back on Leonardo's remarkable letter. Here are some excerpts to give you the flavor:

Having, most illustrious lord, seen and considered the experiments of all those who pose as masters in the art of inventing instruments of war, and finding that their inventions differ in no way from those in common use, I am emboldened, without prejudice to anyone, to solicit an appointment of acquainting your Excellency with certain of my secrets.

1. *I can construct bridges which are very light and strong and very portable . . .*
2. *In case of a siege I can cut off water from the trenches and make pontoons and scaling ladders . . .*
3. *If by reason of the elevation or the strength of its position a place cannot be bombarded, I can demolish every fortress . . .*
4. *I can also make a kind of cannon which is light*

and easy of transport, with which to hurl small stones like hail . . .

5. *I can noiselessly construct to any prescribed point subterranean passages . . .*

10. *In time of peace, I believe that I can give you as complete satisfaction as anyone else in the construction of buildings both public and private, and in conducting water from one place to another.*

I can further execute sculpture in marble, bronze or clay, also in painting I can do as much as anyone else, whoever he may be.

Moreover, I would undertake the commission of the bronze horse, which is to be to the immortal glory and eternal honour of the auspicious memory of your father and of the illustrious house of Sforza.

And if any of the aforesaid things should seem to anyone impossible or impracticable, I offer myself as ready to make trial of them in your park or in whatever place shall please your Excellency, to whom I commend myself with all possible humility.

Leonardo da Vinci

In 1482, the smart way to create a fan club was to earn an appointment with a powerful prince, win that prince's enduring admiration and love, and gain his entire court as your fans. Leonardo did not tell the duke of Milan that his flying machine had design problems or that he had issues to work out with the patina he was experimenting on for his painting. He told the duke that he was smart, successful, enthusiastic, and ready to achieve greatness. He just needed someone to say: Go for it!

The same is true for everyone who would be a high achiever: We need encouragement, friendship, support, and love.

Reaching out for help is not a sign of weakness. It's a celebration of strength. Once the individuals around you understand that you are open to their involvement in your mission, they will be eager to become fan club members. My fan club has been an interesting and effective part of my success as I work through the challenges and frustrations of losing weight and fulfilling my mission. My fan club has more than five hundred active members from all over the world. Some are family and friends, some business contacts and associates. Donald Trump is part of my fan club. So is Muhammad Ali. And I credit Donald and Muhammad and the 498 other members with helping me change my life. I hope some of them found my occasional e-mails helpful to them, as well, in framing their own challenges.

An important aspect of building your fan club is to keep in mind that people are busy and flooded with e-mails all the time, just as you are. You don't want to burden your friends. The goal can never be to try to turn your problems or issues into *their* problems or issues. I always keep e-mails to my fan club short and easy to digest, make clear that I do not demand or expect an answer, and wait until I have real news to impart. You don't want to take advantage of the good nature of the people in your fan club or overtax their patience; these people are very important to you and your mission. When you embark on a major project of personal change and end up falling short and disappointing your family members and closest friends, they are always in the end going to forgive you because they love you. However, you can't expect the same leniency from a fan club. Not letting your fans down becomes almost a mission in and of itself. They are not going to be so quick or willing to forgive as your family members and inner circle. Your intense desire not to be seen as a failure in their eyes can be a huge motivator.

One of the best parts of having a fan club is that it gives you the chance to become a fan yourself. Ted Waitt, the founder and former chairman of Gateway, was one of the five hundred fans I e-mailed with regular updates on how many pounds I had dropped. As I made progress, people sent encouraging e-mails back. Sometimes those responses were as simple as "Great job!" and "Can't wait to see you!" Encouragement does not need to be verbose! Ted sent me one of my favorite e-mails. He complimented me on my progress and then told me about the positive steps he had taken in his own life.

"I quit smoking and cut off my ponytail," Ted told me. That day, I joined the Ted Waitt Fan Club.

CHAPTER 22

Shock and Awe

THE ABILITY TO PEEL away unnecessary or unneeded layers in life has never been more important. The flip side of such empowerment is the real risk of being reactive instead of proactive, of letting inertia rule. That was the direction I was headed when I weighed 406 pounds. Once you pull back the screen on yourself and get a clear and penetrating look at who you are and how you are living, the vision might burn a little, your eyes might water some, but I encourage you to blink back those tears, take a deep breath, and take the plunge forward.

In the 2008 presidential election we heard a lot of talk about being a maverick. Well, I'm a maverick, and I'm betting you are one, or would like to be one, too. What exactly *is* a maverick? It's someone who goes his or her own way and does his or her own thing. One definition in *Merriam-Webster* is "an independent individual who does not go along with a group or party." But what does that really mean?

The original maverick was a Texas land speculator named Samuel Augustus Maverick, who was born in South Carolina in 1803 and studied law. Here is how Sam Maverick's grandson, Maury Maverick, explained his grandfather's contribution in a June 3, 1929, letter to *Time* magazine: "The word 'Maverick' was originally applied to unbranded cattle, still is," the younger Maverick wrote. "The word now means any person, thing or idea which is unbranded, untagged or unregimented.

"The word came from my grandfather, Samuel A. Maverick, who acquired cattle in 1845, and not branding them for many years people called them 'Maverick's.' Forty-niners carried the word to California, all over the West, travelers to Australia. Then it went around the world. . . . 'Maverick,' if a person, is one whose words, deeds and acts are independent; [who] does not bear the brand of any club, organization, or association. A 'Maverick' cannot be classified."

A maverick can be classified only as a maverick. I've talked about going helium and going tiger. Being a maverick is similar in some respects. The common element is to act on your own sense of where you want to go and what you want to be, and leave all the rest behind. The leaving-behind part of life can be difficult, even daunting. It can be painful. But once the break is made, the rewards come streaming in, starting with a newfound sense of energy and purpose, a newfound sense of mission, and a newfound sense of clarity and direction.

*   *   *

Using the tools of empowerment, especially the tools of branding, to shape how you see yourself and how others see you is essential. Just like they say in real estate, "Location, location, location," I say, in brand management, "Brand, brand, brand."

Having a fan club—people who have a stake in your success and failure—helps to keep you focused on your mission. You want to make a point of showing them, even as you're showing yourself, that you're making big leaps forward, not just baby steps that can be erased or reversed in an instant. My suggestion is that you be a showman! Make an entrance! Initiate what I like to call "shock and awe."

My friend Martha Stewart saw me losing pounds and losing inches and feeling better about myself. Knowing me as she does, she understood that it was important for me to be on the lookout for ways to showcase my progress, to renew my sense of mission by savoring the satisfaction and enjoyment that come with progress. When progress feels like a great leap forward, it gives you a jolt of energy and purpose. You don't feel as if you are just muddling along, making incremental progress.

One Sunday afternoon, I was at Martha's house, out in her backyard, discussing how that year it seemed as if we'd had no spring. Winter had gone to summer. One day it was so cold that frost crackled on the ground under your feet, and the next day new leaves were popping out on trees and the temperatures were in the high seventies. Martha keeps a close eye on her garden, and that year there were some blooms she never saw at all because the plants never sprouted. Martha viewed the weather as a lesson for me.

"Why should people get less acclaim and notice for changing than the seasons do?" she asked me. "Aren't both achievements of nature that deserve to be admired and deserve to inspire awe and wonder?"

Mother Nature knows best. When change is gradual, we are allowed to ease into it, as observers and participants. It comes along slowly and pulls you gently along, as if you're on a slow stroll down a country road. If we'd had a more traditional shifting of the seasons that year, the arrival of summer would have inspired no particular excitement or buzz. It would have been what everyone expected. But that year, whether to confirm what Al Gore has taught us about global warming, or to demonstrate some other factor none of us would ever understand, summer made a big, awe-inspiring entrance. It wowed everyone.

That was when Martha and I decided that I should tailor my clothes down as I lost weight and avoid getting new clothes for as long as possible. That way everyone—most especially myself—would be amazed when I made the switch from my elastic-waisted khaki pants and untucked white shirts, which people saw coming before they saw me, to an all-new wardrobe of tailored suits in much smaller sizes. So I kept my old look, my old style, my old clothes, as long as I could. Friends, or associates would ask me from time to time if I was losing weight, but usually in passing, as if they weren't sure. That is the nature of gradual change.

Want to get noticed? Want to get the credit you deserve

for embarking on great personal change? When you are ready, go for shock and awe. Shock and awe is all about wowing those you know with the new you. It's about getting jaw-dropping, positive, good-for-you attention. When you embark on a truly transformative program to change an aspect of yourself or your life, less can quickly turn into more. If a company is working on relaunching one of its brands, it certainly will not announce to the competition that it is updating its formulas, redesigning its appeal, and going after a new target audience until it is good and ready. So why should you?

Martha said it was better to keep wearing the same clothes until I reached the point where my tailors had run out of options. This would be a beautiful day for me, she predicted. And when that phone call from my tailors came, I found out how right she was.

"*Signore Arnell! Signore Arnell!*" my friend and tailor Giuseppe said. Then I heard a burst of Italian that only an Italian tailor could ever hope to decipher. The gist seemed to be "I cannot make these pants any smaller."

Giuseppe talked to me for a while in bursts of Italian, then put Alfredo, the store manager, on the phone.

"The back pockets have come together," Alfredo said. "It will look like you have one giant pocket across your seat! It is time for new pants."

I had to agree. I was always glad to pioneer a promising new look, but not the mono-pocket. So I finally went out and bought an entirely new wardrobe. And from that day on, whenever I showed up at a business meeting or at the office, people were surprised and wowed by my new appearance. The change was dramatic and impossible to miss. It made me feel terrific, because I'd really done it, and it seemed to make other people feel good as well. My progress offered them a powerful reminder of what we *all* can accomplish in our lives—what the human spirit can will and drive—even after countless false starts and failed efforts, if we just get down to it.

I have to applaud Martha for her wisdom. I unveiled my new look and some new clothes at the very point when I was ready for some good, positive encouragement. It was time for me to hear a couple of *wows!* to keep me going on my mission. It was like skipping spring and going right into summer, fall, and winter all at once.

CHAPTER 23

Embrace Mistakes: They Are How You Learn What *Not* to Do

IN REAL LIFE as in the world of business, many of us fall into the trap of relying too much on the tried-and-true and the uncontroversial. Too often our tendency is to hesitate before plunging boldly ahead with a new idea or in a new direction. But as understandable as this reticence is, as *human* as it is, it can become a straitjacket. It hems us in with a million questions about what *not* to do, rather than helping teach us the art of taking a chance and giving something new and potentially scary a shot. The fear of making a mistake—or even just an obsessive focus on trying to avoid mistakes—takes on a life of its own and can start to become second nature. That is why it's worth tunneling down into your assumptions and preconceptions, and dynamiting your old mind-set when it comes to mistakes. Watch your rigid mind-set go sky-high in a cloud of smoke and a hail of rubble rain down all around you.

Sometimes the words *mistake* and *revelation* are almost synonyms. Was it a "mistake" in 1928 when Sir Alexander Fleming, already known as a brilliant researcher, went off on holiday and carelessly left behind samples of bread in his lab, only to mutter and curse at his own carelessness when he returned and discovered they had grown moldy? Was it still a mistake when he pulled some of the bread samples out of the trash and noticed that one of the molds had inhibited the growth of the bacteria he had been studying? We now view that mistake as a "revelation," for it led to the discovery of penicillin.

I've watched this pattern at work, and I've learned to recognize and apply these same lessons at home as well. It's a shortcoming of corporate culture that so often we inhibit individual initiative and individual responsibility because we demand constant confirmation and direction from higher-ups. No one wants to tick the boss off by doing something that takes him or her by surprise. Companies don't like surprises, in general. That is why they spend millions each year to get qualitative and quantitative feedback from consumers. Companies need to have a large national sampling of consumers or customers saying "Good idea!" before they make decisions. The same is true in our private lives. We often look to others for affirmation before we set out in a new direction.

Individuals go to great lengths to avoid mistakes, and to avoid others noticing their mistakes. But that's the wrong way to think. I want to overturn the apple cart (or, in my case, the orange cart) on that one! Occasional mistakes should be a goal! I see mistakes as signposts along the way toward success:

They tell you're on the right track. They tell you you're taking risks and pushing the boundaries to bring yourself to an exciting new place where the old, tired assumptions no longer apply. Only by taking risks can you ever hope to achieve great accomplishments.

So embrace your mistakes! They will help you vault forward to a new way of looking at life. Mistakes should be embraced as a positive piece of learning. After all, now you know one more thing not to do again.

Orville Wright has always been one of my heroes. He is a perfect embodiment of humans' ability to dream—and to soar! He was the first man to fly or, to put it more precisely, the first man to make a sustained flight in a heavier-than-air, motor-powered machine. He dared to imagine that he and his brother could be the ones to do what had never been done! He thought they could pull the truth out of an old sketch by Leonardo and open a new era in human civilization, simply because he believed in the power of flight. What gall! What chutzpah! What a beautiful mind! What stubborn, gritty determination he had to keep on with his foolish experiments even after he and his brother Wilbur were laughed at time after time.

"If we all worked on the assumption that what is accepted as true is really true, there would be little hope of advance," Orville once said. Those are words to live by.

We take flying for granted now. What must it have been like when no one had ever soared through the clouds with the touch of a throttle? How fantastic it must have seemed when the Wright brothers first lifted off the ground. Orville and

Wilbur never let themselves be derailed by the doubts that might have plagued others. They kept right on plugging away, for years, before their triumph in 1903 over the sand dunes of Kill Devil Hills in North Carolina, four miles south of Kitty Hawk. Each of the brothers took two turns piloting their propeller-driven plane over the dunes. They never let fear of failure slow them down or derail them.

Yes, Orville and Wilbur made all kinds of mistakes. They made more mistakes in a month than most people make in a lifetime. First they worked with kites and gliders, in 1896. They wrote to the Smithsonian Institution in 1899 to gather as much information as they could on the mechanics of flight, and they studied the findings of such figures as Octave Chanute and Samuel Pierpont Langley. Then they set to work designing and test-flying a new style of kite. Crash landings, setbacks, and embarrassment became the norm. But they kept plowing ahead. Each and every mistake taught them something new and brought them that much closer to their goal. They saw temporary setbacks as an integral part of the learning experience. Each mistake pointed the way forward, providing fresh clues about what to do and what not to do.

The *New York Times* noted approvingly, in its coverage of Orville Wright's death in 1948, that visitors to the sand dunes near Kitty Hawk used to marvel at the sight of these two young men from Ohio spending hours going to elaborate lengths to injure themselves as they tested early versions of their kite design. "The real fun came when the kite would suddenly nose down and plow into the sand, perhaps at the very start of the flight, while the operator would hurtle out the front door doubled up into a ball and roll in a cloud of dust and sand down the side of the hill until all momentum had been lost," the paper reported. The brothers endured "hundreds of bruising tumbles and daring flights in their frail gliders" before they made aviation history.

Thomas Edison is another of my heroes. He grew up dyslexic. To me, that just means the wiring of his brain gave him unusual aptitudes and abilities that tended to make him go about things differently than other people. Reading did not come easily to him, and he struggled with tasks that many people find easy. The young Edison, growing up in Michigan, made no secret of his restlessness at school. His teacher grew so frustrated that he called young Thomas "addled"—bringing to an end his career as a student in that school. Thereafter, he was homeschooled by his mother. He had to live through a lot of mistakes. He embarrassed himself in front of other children. But he kept right on asking questions and kept right on doing things his own way. He ended up with more than one thousand patents in his name, a remarkable achievement that goes far beyond inventing the incandescent lightbulb.

"I have not failed," Edison said at one point in his experiments to find a long-burning filament. "I've just found ten thousand ways that don't work."

To me, learning to embrace mistakes is another way of learning to love thinking differently. If you think differently, you're going to fall on your face sometimes. You're going to flop. But you may eventually learn to *fly*—like Orville and

Wilbur, or *shine* with the light of a new idea, like Thomas Edison.

Thinking differently is a highly valued trait. Apple built the entire Apple brand on the slogan created by their communications agency, Chiat Day, "Think Different." So what that Apple has only a small share of the personal computing market. The company created entirely new markets as a result of the iPod, the iPhone, the iTunes store, and now iPad. And an entirely new energy and culture resulted. Some might argue that the small percentage of the market that Apple has grabbed for itself is the small percentage of people who help to make a difference. When all the other computers were beige, the Apple computer was white. While other computer companies were advertising computing speeds, Apple was showcasing vintage photographs of people who had thought different. Fast-forward a few years and Apple has continued to "think different" while its competitors have all scrambled to do their best to "think like Apple."

I keep my MacBook Air, iPhone, and iPod near at hand most of the time. The elegant ease of computing, as any Apple user will tell you, does more than free you to focus more of your creative energy on a given problem, rather than grumbling about a bad operating system. The Apple vision rubs off on you and gives you the feeling of being part of a wave of creativity and fun.

The iPod is a great example of thinking different. It is elegant and beautiful yet functional. Steve Jobs decided from the get-go to place a major emphasis on design. He wanted the iPod to be consumer-friendly, as manifested in the simplicity of the device. Apple thought forward; it understood the importance of tying in the hardware of the iPod with easy-to-access content and software. And so it developed iTunes. Apple understood that the iPod could be a home run, but only if there was easy-to-access content that would drive sales of the iPod. Unlike companies with earlier MP3 players, Apple understood the dissatisfaction consumers had with purchasing music. Apple allowed consumers to easily sync up their iPods with its easy-to-use software from home, to sample music before purchasing, and to cherry-pick songs without having to buy a whole album—all for 99¢. Sony and Microsoft are still scrambling to catch up.

Apple is just one example of a company that is pointing the way forward.

As you embark on your own personal change, keep these examples in mind. And keep their mistakes in mind. It's a given that if you dare to make major changes in your life, you're going to have some bad days. You're going to have times when you feel like you've made a mistake that has undermined your progress, and maybe you have. Some mistakes can genuinely set you back. But most can be overcome. Expect to make a mistake or two along the way. Embrace those mistakes as signs that you're moving forward.

CHAPTER 24

One Life

I BELIEVE IT'S TIME to end the work-life separation that so many of us use to erect artificial barriers in our lives. To me, it's this simple: Home Life and Work Life = One Life. What living "One Life" really means is that both business and personal aspects of our life need to be brought together, in harmony. Traditionally, too much work is thought to take away too much personal time and, conversely, rigid personal time is often blamed for interfering with work. Having a singular attitude that is about living your life as one experience, including moving all its parts and pieces together with thoughtfulness and flexibility, allows us to create a powerful momentum.

I'm not saying that compartmentalizing life in the traditional way isn't useful at times. It allows us to shift our behavior from one situation to another. It gives us an excuse for having dessert because we're at a business dinner and everyone else ordered dessert and we don't want to stand out. It gives us an excuse for skipping the gym or going on a shopping binge or indulging in other activities that have prominent places on our what-not-to-do lists. Compartmentalizing provides built-in excuses for all sorts of behavior.

I believe, however, that by living One Life, we can live the best life. Time does not stop because we have a business meeting or a family engagement. It keeps moving forward, and our goals can fall further and further behind if we compartmentalize.

In brand development we utilize concurrent engineering: We get a lot of people fired up at once and get multiple approaches moving forward at the same time in parallel. Not surprisingly, traditional brand development is a *sequential* process. Step one: Learn about consumer behavior. Step two: Create designs and products based on what was learned. Step three: After creating a new product or design, see if it can be made for less. In contrast, the *concurrent* process encourages us to learn, design, and work to improve the supply chain all at once, and to meet at points during the journey to check in with one another to share progress. Its advocates—and I'm one—think concurrent engineering is faster, fosters more innovative thinking, and encourages teams to take responsibility for their output regardless of what came before.

Life itself is a concurrent process. We thrust ourselves into change through multiple approaches that are often launched all at once. So my advice is to stop compartmentalizing. Instead of saying to yourself, "Once I lose ten pounds, I'll start going to the gym," why not start the diet and start going to the gym at the same time? Concurrent, not sequential. These two activities—dieting and working out—are not intertwined; one is not dependent on the other. Instead of telling yourself, "I'll quit smoking after things slow down at work," why not take steps to quit smoking now? But at the same time, start trying to organize your work life to remove as much stress as possible. There's nothing more positive than moving forward. The highest level of stress comes from no-action. From not doing anything. In the concurrent model, one event fuels and inspires another. Compartmentalizing life is like constantly sitting in a waiting room: You're waiting to see the doctor so you can begin to get better.

CHAPTER 2 5

About and Out

THE TECHNOLOGICAL and Star-Trekian tools that have in-
fused our lives, making so much possible that was previously
not even thinkable, have also shackled us. If we can down-
load pictures of a far-off place, it's almost like going there,
right? If we can read articles from newspapers in five different
languages, including all the latest articles, right up to the hour,
we might believe that we are as well informed as if we had
traveled abroad. If we can sit down to video-conference with
people wherever they are—Tokyo or Beijing or Milan or Kin-
shasa or Bangkok or Mexico City—it's tempting to believe
that we can get everything we need without ever leaving our
homes, offices, or wherever "we" are, be it 35,000 feet in the
air or in the middle of an ocean. Maybe we can—sometimes.
But at other times we'll be missing out, not only on new,

deeper, and richer experiences, but on the chance to show ourselves to the world.

When I got serious about making a new life for myself, I knew I had to break the old rules at every turn. Most of the time when seriously overweight people decide to go on a new diet, they keep a low profile. I decided to do the opposite. I wanted everyone to know what I was doing. It somehow felt great to share the results, as it made me "be thin" already. Other people might hide at home, out of the public eye, as much as possible. That wasn't going to be my approach! In fact, in the early stages of my mission to lose a large amount of weight, I decided to go out to dinner every single night. This strategy may sound counterintuitive, but think about it: It's easy to be careful about what you eat at home when your wife is grilling you vegetables or whipping up some specialized concoction in the blender. But if you hide away, a part of you will always be yearning to get out to your favorite restaurants and order your favorite foods.

So I decided to go to my favorite restaurants every night. I chose my favorites: Da Silvano, Nobu, and Hatsuhana, all first-rate Manhattan restaurants with amazing menus. I went to each one and announced that I was on a diet and from that point forward I would be eating much differently than I had been. I didn't say this sheepishly. I said it proudly. I was feeling good and full of confidence, expecting good things to happen for me. And people seemed to find my attitude inspiring and contagious. Today, I have an expanded repertoire of restaurants that includes The Four Seasons, Sant Ambroeus, and many others, all more than happy to accommodate special requests.

Silvano, the owner of Da Silvano, saw how serious I was and offered to work with me on developing some special new menu items for me. My favorite was the Arnell Salad, a mixture of grilled chicken strips, chickpeas, beets, onions, and tomatoes, an assortment of different lettuces for variety and texture, and a very light vinaigrette dressing. Soon I was like a regular at an old-time corner bar, where the bartender sees you coming and has your favorite cocktail ready for you in no time: I arrived at the restaurant several times a week. Silvano and the waiters greeted me as family, because that's what I was by then, and they prepared my dinner, an Arnell Salad, without ever asking me for my order. A waiter brought it to my table with a great flourish, just as stylishly as if I were having that day's house special. More often than not, it looked so good that people I was eating with—or sometimes people at nearby tables—decided they also wanted Arnell Salads.

Over at Hatsuhana, the head sushi chef, Seki, worked with me to create an array of rice-free sushi rolls, which I loved eating as an alternative to sashimi, which can get tiresome when you eat only sashimi meal after meal. Chef Seki whipped up sushi with seaweed and asparagus and scallions and radish and an assortment of other vegetables, depending on the season and availability, with the best fresh raw fish, providing endless taste and satisfaction. Chef Seki kept a secret recipe book behind the long wooden sushi bar and when I popped in for one of my regular visits, he pulled it out with a smile and took special pride in making me a dinner that was both unique and delicious. This book became a diary of me and my diet, and he ended up giving it to me as a gift.

As I started to drop pounds in a noticeable way, people asked me for my secret to success with my diet. I always said: No secrets. I was open and honest. Often I mentioned how much I enjoyed stopping in at Da Silvano, Nobu, or Hatsuhana and eating off-the-menu specialties the chefs there had developed for me.

"How did you get them to do that for you?" people invariably wanted to know.

"I asked!"

It's important in life to ask for what you want as well as to just share your thoughts. Too often we let shyness or caution or fear hold us back. It's also important to ask for what you want *in the right way*, without embarrassment or hesitation. If you don't ask, you will never know. If you do ask, chances are people will try to accommodate you whenever possible. Ask for help, and then ask for what you want. No need to go into your whole life story.

Example: "I need your help. I am on a special diet."

Asking for help is one of the most powerful tools toward change there is. It means you will never be alone. Really, as you embark on your own mission to make big changes in your life, you will be amazed at how often people will surprise you and be there for you. People will really want to be there for you to offer help and support, if you open yourself up to that opportunity. It's like a potent multiplying effect that can act like rocket engines strapped on to yourself to turbo-charge you toward your goals. But none of it happens if you stay at home, hiding from the world, and don't reach out to others. None of it happens if you keep your goals—and your mission—a secret.

You need people around you, not only the ones you care the most about, but others as well, so they can help you keep your focus and your discipline and your control. Nothing is harder than trying to achieve significant life change by yourself. The only part of the journey you need to perform alone and by yourself is committing to change, because the decision to commit 100 percent for life has to be a decision that you alone make. It can't be one you agree to because the people who love you have needled and threatened and cajoled you into charting a new course. Every other aspect of your mission, however, can and should take place out in the open with the support and involvement of everyone around you.

Change is an invitation. If you create a party, everyone is going to want to be invited. Once people respond to that invitation and have a stake in your progress, they will feel involved—and they will start taking credit for helping you change. That's good! You want them to feel ownership. You want your success and your progress to be their success and their progress, too.

You want a varied fan club. If at all possible, you would like your fan club to comprise a diverse group of people, each person offering different input and a different level of support. I got support from Rune Stokmo, my friend and fellow photographer; Tom Von Essen, former New York City fire commissioner; Lynn Tierney, former president of the Tribute

Center at Ground Zero; and Tom Dowd, a longtime client and friend. Each had his or her own contribution to make to my progress.

Rune Stokmo told me: *Anything you want or need, just ask and I will make it happen.* That was the kind of unconditional support he offered.

Tom Von Essen said: *I'll be there to remind you of your kids, your family, your friends, all the people that count on you and love you, to remind you of all you have to live for.* That was his offer of support.

Lynn Tierney told me: *I feel your pain; we're in this together.* Her compassion was real and moving.

Tom Dowd said: *I will go shopping with you for food and work with a chef who can make you meals when you travel. I will go to the gym with you and work out with you.*

Silvano will tell you that *he* was the one who made the difference in me finally losing so much weight. Chef Seki feels that *he* was the one. Both are right. Rune Stokmo feels that *he* was the one to help me get there, and he takes credit. Tom Von Essen and Lynn Tierney and Tom Dowd and dozens of other friends all take credit for my transformation. And they deserve it, too. It takes a village! You need friends, associates, and family to turn your quest for major personal change into a great group happening. They makes the journey more enjoyable and make you more likely to succeed.

My friend Marisa Marchetto, Silvano's wife, is a cancer vixen. No, that's not a typo—I mean "cancer vixen." That's exactly what Marisa is. She even has a book out called *Cancer Vixen*, a graphic novel that *Time* called "as good as the best *Sex and the City* episodes." Marisa learned she had breast cancer, and she wasn't about to let it change who she was—as she put it, a "shoe-crazy, lipstick-obsessed, wine-swilling, pasta-slurping, fashion-fanatic, single-forever, about-to-get-married big-city girl cartoonist with a fabulous life."

She decided to fight the disease. She said, "Cancer, I'm going to kick your butt and I'm going to do it in five-inch heels!" She was not about to let cancer turn her into a gloomy, gray figure doing her best to lose herself in a crowd. Just the opposite! She dressed up and pulled out her favorite pair of shoes for her chemo sessions. She wore bold headscarves and designer clothes that said "Look at me!" She went out to dinner, out on shopping sprees, and of course out to parties and clubs. She was determined not to give up who she had been before her diagnosis. That is something people often do. Marisa resisted the temptation to classify life moments as "before cancer" or "after cancer." She wore five-inch heels before the diagnosis; after the battle with cancer started, she wore five-inch heels; and she's still wearing five-inch heels.

Along the way she didn't try to keep her cancer a secret from friends. She reached out to them for their love, support, and attention and made them part of her positive approach to a potentially terrifying time of her life. She did not shrink from public view. She wanted to be out and about. She wanted to be seen, to share her pain and her joy with the world, with her friends and family, and that was inspiring. Marisa beat back her cancer and did it with a click of her heels and a grin. Her story is a wonderful example of why it's a great idea to get out there, to mix with the world, when you are going through an important transition.

We all feel an impulse sometimes to hide. We want the world to go away. But like Marisa, we can demand that the world take us on our own terms, and in so doing, we make our vision of ourselves bolder and stronger and more durable. The lesson is that a drastic life change does not necessarily mean you have to lose the parts of yourself that you like or that define you or your style.

Keeping your personal issues private is not always the best way to go. I really believe that most of the people you come in contact with in your everyday life want to help you. They want to be on your side. They want to be supportive. This is human nature at its most generous and best, humanity in its finest expression. During my time of major transition, I never ceased to be amazed at the support and goodwill and solidarity I encountered when opening up to people. They came from surprising directions and were empowering and energizing. I've already mentioned the friends and others who joined in my quest as members of my fan club; they were vitally important to me. So, too, were strangers and acquaintances I saw in the street or on an elevator ride. Don't count anyone out as a source of comfort and support!

Telling people what is happening with you, even if that feels uncomfortable, and involving them in your life is honest and real. Telling it like it is means you are living openly in the here and now. When you try to hide the truth about who you are and what you hope to be, or what you are facing, you're hiding it from yourself.

There has to be a better way to deal with problems and issues honestly and simply than sheepishly "admitting" to them. If you want to change your life, the last thing you need to be is apologetic. *Acknowledge* problems and issues. *Acknowledging* is proactive and positive. Get it out there, in public, and get on with what you want to do. Keeping secrets is exhausting. You don't need that! You need to move forward.

More than 100 million bloggers go online to share their thoughts about their lives and their loves, their problems and their dreams, or hundreds of other passions or topics. People want to express, connect, and find common likes and goals in order to feel part of a greater being. A new weblog is created every second, and the number of blogs doubles every five months. Blogs allow for instant, interactive dialogue with anyone who is interested in a given subject, like-minded or not. Facebook and other sites that bring people together provide a great platform for individuals to reinvent or identify themselves. Your photo, your opinions, your tone, and your style all speak to your brand.

Blogging allows personal brand expression, a way to elevate yourself from individual to institution. It goes beyond style to substance. In fact, it makes substance the new indicator of style. When Marisa was fighting her breast cancer, her style was as much about looking great in five-inch heels as it was about a bold, outward expression of strength and commitment to wage her personal fight and in the end to triumph.

The Japanese have a great expression, *Genchi Genbutsu*, which means "Go and see for yourself." That phrase has acquired a certain cachet in management circles, because managers typically want to get out and see what's going on. But I think the phrase can take us much farther than that. I mentioned the *Pietà* in Saint Peter's Basilica in the Vatican. If your interest was piqued, I hope you'll consider seeing for yourself—traveling to Rome or going online for information or buying a book about Michelangelo and reading about his art and technique. In other words, I hope you'll take action, building on my introduction to his work and letting it open up new worlds for you.

Shout About It

I AM DOING MY BEST to share my insights with you, give you proof, and implore you to believe in my passion and take my urgency into your heart and mind. I am doing my best to impart to you my conviction that we must work vigorously to avoid getting stuck in quagmires of disinterest and ambivalence. Why not yearn to ascend the towering peaks that represent dreams made real and aspirations given life? Powerful words, yes, but the point here is to focus not on how to express an idea, but on how to *live* an idea, how to live change, how to Shift. How to create a new you, whatever new you might float on the near horizon.

Once you've done that—really done it—you will find that living your new life is not enough. You need to share the new you with others, so that they may benefit from your experiences. After all, it was the people in your fan club and so many others who helped get you over and *beyond* the hump. So nothing makes more sense than going on a mission to inspire others with the same ferocity and imagination that you have. Being a better person requires the generosity of spirit to help other people with what you have learned, not only your close friends and family members, but all the people who you come in contact with in life and in work.

Not long ago I was in Los Angeles on business. My driver for the day was a big overweight guy whom I gave the affectionate nickname, for a reason I can't remember anymore, "Tony the Dog." I sat in the back of the car and kept my eye on him as he drove me to various meetings, and after a few days of this, I finally decided I had to say something to this man.

"Tony, are you interested in losing weight?"

His first reaction was shock. He was surprised I had been so straightforward. Slim and trim and well dressed, I sat in the back of the limo and watched his face to wait for the shock to run its course.

Tony glanced into the rearview mirror and saw me smiling in a friendly, open, encouraging way.

"Would you believe me if I told you I lost 256 pounds?" I asked.

I had his attention then.

"No lie," I told Tony. "No bullshit."

Then we got to talking. Tony opened right up and told me he badly wanted to lose weight. He thought about it all the time, every day, as he sat at the wheel of the limo, the steering wheel rubbing against his stomach because he was too big to fit into the space allotted. His problem, he told me, was his wife. She was too good a cook. He loved her food so much, he couldn't stop until he'd filled up on it.

This is an excuse I hear often. I could have stopped myself with the same excuse: I could have said the food at Da Silvano is way too good! How can a man lose weight with dishes like that? Instead, I got to work on making the changes necessary to make a new life and a new me.

As I explained all this to Tony, I told him he should start his own fan club to help keep himself focused on the challenge at hand. I offered to join his fan club, and I did. And almost every month I receive an e-mail from Tony in L.A., a man I barely know but a man whose life is connected to mine. Tony is making progress. The last I heard, he had dropped 20 pounds and was a lot more comfortable sitting behind the wheel of the limo. It was a great beginning. But he wanted to lose more. He wanted to make it to 25 pounds. "Make it 50!" I e-mailed back. Insulting? No—as exhilarating as helium.

If you're in your thirties or forties or older and you've been living in New York, chances are you've heard of Crazy Eddie. You might not know how or where you heard the name, but it probably sounds somewhat familiar. In 1972, the owners of a family-owned chain of consumer electronics stores made a name for their business with a series of TV and radio commercials that were so high-energy, so unforgettable, that they were a sensation in the New York area for the next two decades. The chain's name was Crazy Eddie, and the owners were the Antar family, Jewish immigrants from Aleppo, Syria. The Antars were looking for an edge, something to single their company out in the crowded consumer electronics market.

Their chance came when "Dr. Jerry," aka Jerry Carroll, a DJ on WPIX-FM, read a live commercial for Crazy Eddie and at the end ad-libbed, "Crazy Eddie, his prices are IN-SA-A-A-A-A-ANE!" Carroll's crazy voice and delivery transformed the line into an instant classic. Eddie Antar called Carroll right away and hired him to read the spot that way every time. Soon the New York airwaves were filled with Crazy Eddie spots, all featuring Carroll, and business boomed. At its peak, Crazy Eddie had more than forty stores and was pulling in more than $300 million in sales annually. In movies from the 1970s or 1980s shot in New York, you'll sometimes see or hear a Crazy Eddie commercial.

The Antar family understood that if you keep quiet, you will quickly be forgotten. Even twenty years after Crazy Eddie went bankrupt as a result of financial improprieties, anyone who saw or heard the commercials about the "IN-SA-A-A-A-ANE" deals can still remember those ads. There are tribute Web sites dedicated to Crazy Eddie and its screaming pitchman. "His stare was maniacal, his voice boomed, he flailed his arms about, and we loved it!" A bankrupt brand with a cult following is definitely something to scream about.

My point? Sometimes shouting isn't all bad. The energy and excitement of raising your voice and speaking with conviction causes your heartbeat to increase and your blood pressure to shoot up. Your adrenaline surges. Even if you aren't exercising your vocal chords, shouting about something figuratively—telling people your good news—can inject into any conversation all the excitement and energy of a full-fledged scream. Passionate oratory does the same thing to your body as yelling. It gets the blood going. And that is why in helping others, you can continue to help yourself as well.

Bill Clinton understands that very well. Since leaving office, the former president has raised billions of dollars for charity work around the globe. He is the U.N.'s Special Envoy to Haiti and helped during the earthquake disaster, a supporter of Special Olympics, and, through his foundation, a provider to many causes. One of his big issues is fighting AIDS and HIV in Africa. As almost everyone remembers from Clinton's years in the White House, he was a regular jogger and struggled with his weight. In 2004 he had major heart surgery, followed by serious complications, all of which forced him to alter his diet radically. Today he is actively involved in the issue of childhood obesity and is always looking for new ways to get his message across—even shouting.

In October 2006 I was in the crowd at a grade school in Harlem when Bill Clinton came to speak. Clinton was up front with top executives from Kraft Food, Mars, PepsiCo, and Campbell Soup to talk about the need for better nutrition in schools, and for a stronger effort against poor eating habits among the young. Clinton announced that his organization, Alliance for a Healthier Generation, planned to work with all of those major companies to provide healthier, more nutritious snacks for schoolchildren.

Reporters, as usual, were at first skeptical that this program could have any impact. One reporter asked the former president why he thought that simply better eating habits could make a big enough difference and if it could really help in the fight against obesity.

President Clinton called out to me, microphone in hand. "I'm going to embarrass you now. Peter, stand up." I stood up.

Clinton looked around the room briefly.

"When I first met Peter a few years ago, he weighed 356 pounds," the president said. "Now he is 150 pounds—and he doesn't even have any stretch marks."

There were murmurs in the crowd, and applause.

"He didn't want to die, so he changed his life," Clinton said.

That's an example of what I mean by shouting about it. Do not be afraid to proclaim a positive example so that others might benefit from it. This type of "shouting" worked for President Clinton, and it has worked for me. It will work for you, too.

"Shouting" isn't always about being loud. Do not be afraid to be loud if that's where your message is taking you. But "shouting" can be done quietly. It is about taking pride in achievement, and pride in making something happen for yourself and for others in a way that can help and inspire them. You can "shout" to yourself as well as to others by leaving a Post-it Note on the fridge, or coming up with some other visual reminder of a recent achievement. Those are ways to encourage yourself to greater heights.

Talking openly and positively about what you've accomplished so others can learn is also "shouting." Sometimes a life change is something people wish to keep private. Millions of people never knew me as an obese person. I don't need to tell new clients or acquaintances that I was once overweight. I don't need to tell them that I didn't take care of myself and was unable to control my obsession with food. But, in fact, I share this information about myself every chance I can.

I share it with people who want to benefit from hearing about the struggle and the success. Change is hard. Sometimes you need a guide, and that's why I "shout" about it, not to brag or to find a cathartic release, but to broadcast hope. And even if I am broadcasting to someone who is not on a path to great personal change, chances are that person knows someone who is, a friend or family member, and might be able to pass on the message. It's like creating a chain letter. It gets around, and if you believe, you send it out to five friends. If you don't believe, you hit "delete." I give people the opportunity to opt in or to opt out. When you're ready, when you have your own story of personal change to share with the world, it will be time for you to do the same.

Making *Our* Place in History

I LOVE TO GO FOR LONG WALKS in New York early in the morning. It's a great way to think a problem through or to empty my mind of distractions and wait for a good idea to come. Often, I stop at the Trinity Churchyard cemetery downtown. It's a beautiful church with a beautiful little graveyard, at the corner of Wall Street and Broadway. All day long people rush by without taking a second look. I stand there and look at the grave of Alexander Hamilton and am amazed that no one so much as pauses to cast a respectful glance at the final resting place of one of the most important of our nation's founders. How could so many have forgotten that Hamilton was our first secretary of the treasury? That he was aide-de-camp to General George Washington during the Revolutionary War? That he died after being mortally wounded in a duel with Aaron Burr across the Hudson River in New Jersey?

To me, Hamilton's grave is a shrine to progress, to culture, to freedom—freedom in the sense of liberty, and also personal freedom, the freedom to choose greatness, the freedom to summon from deep within the bravery and conviction to live life as we choose to live it. That's my religion. That's aiming high, I know. But if we don't aim high for ourselves, who can we do that for? When I stop and stare at the elegant, understated headstone on Hamilton's grave, I feel time slow, I feel my pulse quicken, and I feel a sense of awe and responsibility and hope welling up around me. The headstone reads,

> *In Testimony of Their Respect*
> *FOR*
> *The PATRIOT of incorruptible INTEGRITY.*
> *The SOLDIER of approved VALOUR.*
> *The STATESMAN of consummate WISDOM:*
> *Whose TALENTS and VIRTUES will be admired*
> *Long after this MARBLE shall have mouldered into*
> *DUST*

The word *dust* stands alone on the stone, in the middle of the next-to-last line. It is followed only by "He died July 12th, 1804, aged 47."

"We are not always sure that those who advocate the truth are influenced by purer principles than their antagonists," Hamilton wrote in *The Federalist*, No. 1. "Ambition, avarice, personal animosity, party opposition, and many other motives, not more laudable than these, are apt to operate as well upon those who support as upon those who oppose the right side of a question. Were there not even these inducements to moderation, nothing could be more illjudged than that intolerant spirit which has, at all times, characterized political parties. For, in politics as in religion, it is equally absurd to aim at making proselytes by fire and sword." This quote always gets me thinking about truth and principles.

I think of those words as I stand contemplating the tranquillity that always surrounds his grave. Sometimes I stay for half an hour or more, ideas jumping in my head like trout in a stream. And in that time thousands of people may pass by with no idea of the piece of American history they are missing.

Sooner or later, we are all going to end up in the grave. How would you like to remember your life, looking back from the calm and quiet of your eternal resting place? Will you be able to look back and know that you put your back into living the way you wanted to live, no matter what the obstacles, no matter the state of the economy or the job market or the housing market or your 401(k) account? Will you be able to look back with the satisfaction of knowing that you challenged yourself, stripped away your fears, and dared to plunge into life to become who you were meant to be?

I'm hoping to be able to say yes. For me that view of Hamilton gives me a deep sense of calm and confidence: We can make our own history, in the here and now. We can stand astride the currents of history and the currents of our life and not merely be pushed along by events like flotsam and jetsam carried along by a swift current. We can be the drivers of our destiny.

Spoken in a vacuum, words like that sound dramatic and

overblown. But I'm not speaking in a vacuum. I have shared some painful details of my own life, my own past struggles with my weight and all that entailed. I've tried to cull from my own experiences, in my private life and in my work life (remember: It's all one life!), to help you gain more leverage for change in your own life.

I've described various tactics that work. I'm excited that now you get to go out there and try them and discover your own. Everyone's approach will be unique; I can only encourage you down the path to change. So let me take a last look at Hamilton's grave, a final reminder of the greatness that resides in all of us. Embark on your own path toward making a new life. Do me that favor. You owe it to yourself. Now, get started! SHIFT!

Acknowledgments

I would like to thank my family, friends, and colleagues who have provided undying loyalty and dedication . . . from the bottom of my heart.

Index

INDEX

204

About the Authors

PETER ARNELL is the founder and chairman of Arnell, a design, branding, and communications company in New York City. He founded this business in 1979, after working in the office of the architect Michael Graves. He has written, edited, and designed academic monographs on architects that include Frank Gehry, Aldo Rossi, Robert A.M. Stern, and Michael Graves. He collaborated with the artist David Hockney on *Cameraworks,* with Paul Goldberger on *The Houses of the Hamptons,* and with Robert Venturi and Denise Scott Brown on *A View from the Campidoglio.* His design work has won many awards, including the 2007 gold medal IDEA from *Business Week* for the HomeHero fire extinguisher, the Cannes Gold Lion for best in category for communications, and the first Council of Fashion Designers of America Award in 1987 for excellence in branding and communications. He has received the Harlem Renaissance Award, the F.I.T. Alumni Star Salute award, and the Ellis Island Medal of Honor. He is a board member of the Special Olympics and an honorary fire commissioner of the Fire Department of the City of New York, where he also serves as the chief creative officer for fire safety and recruitment communications. Arnell was born in Brooklyn, New York, the grandson of immigrants Nathan and

Ada Hutt. He lives in Westchester County, New York, with his family.

STEVE KETTMANN, an author and journalist based in Berlin, is a political columnist for the *Berliner Zeitung* and has reported for the *New York Times*, the *Los Angeles Times*, *GQ*, *Parade*, the *New Republic*, *Washington Monthly*, and many other publications. The author of *One Day at Fenway*, about one game between the Yankees and the Red Sox, Kettmann has cowritten the number-one bestsellers *Juiced* (with Jose Canseco) and *What a Party!* (with Terry McAuliffe).